WHEN *Life* CHANGES FOREVER

WHEN *Life* CHANGES FOREVER

dealing with it...

SUSAN M. BIGLIONE & MARTHA E. LAISNE

TATE PUBLISHING & Enterprises

Published by Tate Publishing & Enterprises, LLC
127 E. Trade Center Terrace | Mustang, Oklahoma 73064 USA
1.888.361.9473 | www.tatepublishing.com

Tate Publishing is committed to excellence in the publishing industry. The company reflects the philosophy established by the founders, based on Psalm 68:11,
"The Lord gave the word and great was the company of those who published it."

Book design copyright © 2008 by Tate Publishing, LLC. All rights reserved.
Cover design by Tate Publishing
Interior design by Kandi Evans

Published in the United States of America

ISBN: 978-1-60462-258-4
1. References: Personal & Practical
08.04.22

To Donna Dotson,

the inspiration for this book.

TABLE OF *Contents*

Chapter 4: Insurance

Chapter 5: Legal

QUICK *Reference Guide*

Acknowledgments

Just, of course, when you need them the most, words fail to express the depth of my gratitude to friends and acquaintances for their love and generosity. I am indebted to so many friends who embraced my idea, enthusiastically contributed ideas, and encouraged me. I am particularly grateful to all who took the extra steps and offered their skill, expertise, time, and friendship.

To my husband, Fred, whose love is the essence of my life, who encouraged and endured the production of this book, and makes everything in my life possible. To my precious friend, Donna; you are my inspiration and the reason for this book. To Anne, whose encouragement and approval inspires me. To Diana, you are my rock. To the "Ripe Tomatoes," my lunch companions, for their support and motivation, and the Fig Garden Women's Club who have always been there for me.

And last but not least, my beloved, talented, and gifted sister, Martha, who so patiently took my notes, rewrote them, and gave them life.

Thank you for all your gifts; the ones I read in the margins of many unfinished drafts and the unwritten ones that I am touched by every day.

I have been truly blessed.
Susan M. Biglione

Each person touches our lives and shapes how we view the world and live in it. I am privileged to live and work among a community that encourages and reflects the very best in us. I am especially grateful to Steve and Traudy Bradley for enduring friendship; Rita Colella for unfailing enthusiasm; and Cathyjean and Doug Gustafson for generous contributions. My thanks to all HBSers. For my dear sister, Susan, coauthor and mentor, who taught me the real power of love (and tolerated my obstreperousness with grace, cheer, and steel), I am deeply grateful. For myriad reasons, I am profoundly grateful for and indebted to my son, teacher, and best friend, Gene. To each of our brave sons and daughters of the Armed Forces who give us the most cherished gift of all, thank you.

Martha E. Laisné

INTRODUCTION

When Life Changes Forever focuses on life's experiences: those fragile moments when life, for *you*, changes forever because of some extraordinary event.

For a fortunate few, life goes smoothly; they get an education, begin a career, marry, raise children, retire to a leisurely lifestyle, and die peacefully. For many others the reality is quite different; a mid- or late-life divorce, catastrophic illness or injury, the premature death of a spouse or child, or any other unwelcome and unexpected crisis, alters life dramatically and forever.

When crises occur, we are often unprepared to deal with their realities. At these moments we are set adrift in a world we no longer comprehend and called upon to make decisions on matters we may know little about, much less how they will impact our lives years into the future. "What am I going to do?" we ask. It is not a simple question. Where do we get help? Family? Sure. Friends? Yes. Professionals? Absolutely. But what professionals, and are family and friends knowledgeable in the areas in which we need help? Maybe. Maybe not.

At a time when your only goal may be to just survive the next hour, you must make decisions that are as important to you as they are to your family and loved ones. With basic information you can begin to manage and improve your circumstances quickly, when time is not on your side. Most of us don't need, or want, to know everything about a particular subject; all the knowledge in the world about, say, finances, won't give us a clue about how to deal with health care issues. It's not rocket science; it will take some time and effort, but it is not impossible and *you can do it.*

If you've been running a household and/or a small business, there isn't much more we, or anyone else, can tell you about money and how to use it. If you're a single parent, you know more about organization and economics than most CEOs or PhDs. For those who have not dealt with personal crises or life-altering events and anyone who has not prepared for their future, *When Life Changes Forever* offers useful starting points in unfamiliar territory much like a roadmap helps the traveler. We do not presume to give advice; this is not a "how-to" book. The questions we address are those we have asked or wish we had. Each situation is different; the choices you make are yours. Our aim is to ease your stress by suggesting in clear, common sense language, routes you may choose to suit your needs.

All of your issues can be dealt with in a timely manner, but you cannot make rational decisions until you understand what you're dealing with. Your *Life*

File will be your lifeline. If you have all the information and documents you need at your fingertips, you can answer questions and make decisions. With your *Life File* and *When Life Changes Forever,* you can prepare for unexpected events and find the information you need to make the best decisions for you and your family.

Our journey begins by defining the playing field, six broad areas: family, finance, medical, insurance, legal, and retirement. Certainly each of these areas is far too complicated for a single chapter, or, indeed, a single book. The focus of *When Life Changes Forever* is the fundamentals of preparing to deal with unexpected events in these areas. In *Chapter 1, Family,* issues for new and old families are presented; for example, organizing personal papers (and what they are) in a *Life File* and creating emergency communication plans. *Chapter 2, Finance,* focuses on credit, identity theft and how to deal with it, and financial tools and planning. *Chapter 3, Medical,* defines some medical terms, health care proxies, care facilities, and assistance programs. *Chapter 4, Insurance,* reviews various policy types and medical benefits programs. Legal issues, such as powers of attorney, wills, and trusts are discussed in *Chapter 5, Legal.* In addition, the practical aspects of coping with death are reviewed. Finally, *Chapter 6, Retirement,* contains information on pensions and retirement savings plans, veteran's programs, and budgets. Budgets are included in this chapter on the theory that it is at retirement that most people tighten their belts but feel free to use the budget information and form at any time.

A *Quick Reference Guide* follows the *Table of Contents* at the beginning of the text and a *Glossary of Terms* that often contains additional information than presented in the text, is located at the end of the book. Not one other person on this planet will truly understand your situation, but there are many who are willing and able to help; the *Resource Directory* lists some.

None of what is included here is too complicated or too mysterious for most of us to understand when it is clearly explained. It's not brain surgery; it's life, and we're human beings that every now and then need a little help. Never underestimate yourself; get as much information as possible and make the best decisions you can; it's all that can be expected of anyone and more than most will do.

Most of all, we offer encouragement. We hope *When Life Changes Forever* reduces your anxiety by proposing routes to answering your questions and finding the help you need. You've taken the first step; let's take the next ones together.

With our sincerest best wishes, we are,
Susan M. Biglione
Martha E. Laisné

CHAPTER 1: *Family*

YOUR FIRST AID:
A PLAN FOR THE UNPLANNED

When Life Changes Forever is about making life easier for you. It is not a "how-to" book, and we do not presume to offer advice. Every day we meet new challenges, small or large: a flat tire on the way to work; an unexpected interruption of work; an illness or death. How we cope with these situations defines who we are and forever changes the way we face life. Each trial broadens our experience and helps us deal with new obstacles based on the sure knowledge gained from previous experiences.

For most people, a flat tire or a cold are minor inconveniences. Mercifully, most people only face a few life-altering situations in a lifetime. But a trip to the hospital, for example, for anyone, for any reason, is cause for anxiety. This may also be true when visiting an attorney's office, a bank, or a government agency. *When Life Changes Forever* is not about health care or financial or legal issues; it is about how to prepare for them.

In this book we address such questions as: What

do you need to know before you go? What documents will be required and where do you get them? What does the language mean? What resources are available? What are your options?

How often have we gone to a state agency, government office, or bank only to find that we cannot accomplish our errand because we don't have the appropriate documentation or information? You could, of course, call first and you may or may not get the information you need. Are you asking the right questions? If you ask a bank telephone operator about opening a bank account when, in fact, you want to discuss establishing a trust account, you have not asked the correct question and will be directed to an inappropriate area. One of the first questions you will be asked when visiting a hospital is: Do you have a medical proxy or living will? If not, most health care facility personnel will hand you a form to sign. What is it? Are you in any condition to deal with it, or even read it? Being an especially litigious society, are you waiving any rights by signing it?

If we don't know the answers to fundamental questions or how to frame our questions, where do we get this information? The Internet is convenient with tremendous amounts of information—and notoriously unreliable. What is someone's opinion or an ad for a costly service that may or may not be legitimate and able to achieve our goals is not always easy to determine. Other information from reliable sources may be technical and assume a consumer knowledge we do not have. Books are an option. You may buy a book on personal finances, one on insurance, and one on legal issues. Not exactly the essence of convenience. In the larger context, how much of the information in those books will be useful to you?

Katrina screamed her messages loudly and clearly: be self-reliant, be prepared, know what information and documents you need and what you must do in an emergency. Without taking all of your important papers when, for whatever reason, you must leave your home, how long will it take, and how difficult will it be to duplicate them? In an age when no one is exempt from suspicion, in order to duplicate one form of identification, you must produce another. How and where do you begin? What items should you focus on first, which second, and third? To be self-reliant, you must create your own *Life File*.

GET IT TOGETHER

Whether we think about it or not, our first priority is the safety of our family. Every action we take, the schools we choose, the nutritious meals we serve, supervising recreation, and the hundreds of other things we do every day, all protect and keep our family safe. But in spite of all our precautions, accidents happen. Any parent knows that in the blink of an eye, they could be racing a child to the hospital with a broken bone or other injury. It's life and that's how it happens.

Have you taken every step you can to prepare for an emergency? If an emergency involves your home or neighborhood, do you have a list of emergency services handy? Do all family members know where it is and how to react? Some of the simplest steps are to:

* organize important papers in one place;

* display an emergency plan where all family members can access it, or in several places throughout your home;

* program emergency telephone numbers into all cell phones and have a list beside or attached to your landline phone; and

* create a list of medications and health issues of each family member.

This may seem like a lot of information, but you can probably type it all on one page. This is not meant to inspire fear; just the opposite, it is meant to prevent fear and panic and instill a sense of safety and security in your home.

During difficult situations, organizing (or perhaps even finding) personal papers is simply not possible. If you don't have the luxury of time, refer to the *Quick Reference Guide* and come back here later. Organizing documents for quick access and having them all in one place is critical. How frustrating is it when you can't lay your hands on a document when there is no emergency? Multiply that anxiety level by a thousand in an emergency. If you don't organize your papers now, what are the chances you'll do it later, and will later be too late?

If you're single, organizing your personal papers may be relatively easy. If you're married there may be more involved. Even if you're not particularly fond of paperwork, it's a task that needs to be done and you'll be surprised at how much you learn in the process. The bright side is that it's a one-time project; once it's done all you have to do is update. It is a stressful waste of time to be guessing at your situation when you must know.

YOUR LIFE FILE

To begin, buy a file box (we call it a *Life File*) at a stationery store, Wal-Mart, Target, or a grocery store. Also buy file folders and invest in a shredder. A shredder may seem a little over-the-top, but why risk it? Crooks dumpster dive for a living; don't let their living be at your expense. And you don't need the Cadillac model of shredders; it is, after all, a pair of scissors.

Label the *Life File* folders with the following topics:

1. Family

2. Finance

3. Medical

4. Insurance

5. Legal

6. Retirement

Use the suggestions in the table below as a checklist for what to include in your *Life File*. Not everything is appropriate for you; use what you need and add your own information. Make it your own.

Family	Finance
Disaster Plan	Asset List
EmergencyPhone	Automobile Records
Numbers	Banking Information
Family Information	ATM Cards
Social Security Numbers	Credit Cards
Birth Certificates	Credit Bureaus/Credit
Marriage Certificates	Scores
Death Certificates	Credit Unions
Adoption Records	Identity Theft
Naturalization Records	Annuities
Passports	Bonds
Divorce Records	Certificates of Deposit
Alimony Records	Mutual Funds
School Records	Stock Certificates
Safe Combinations	
Computer Passwords	
Professional	
Memberships	

Medical	Insurance

Medical Records
List of Medications
List of Physicians
Medicare
Social Security Benefits
Health Reimbursement
  Accounts
Health Savings Accounts
Durable Power of
  Attorney for
  Health Care
Living Will
	Homeowners and
	  Renters
	Health and Life
	Medigap policies
	Medicare Coverage
	Medicare Coverage
	  Costs

Legal	Retirement
Powers of Attorney Letter of Instruction Will Trusts Death and Coping	Pension Plans Social Security Earnings Limits Veterans Benefits Budgeting

Not everyone has, or needs, all of the items listed in the table, and the papers you need are probably stored in a drawer, desk, or box. Don't be overwhelmed by the list; each item is explained. Pare the list down by crossing out what you don't need or adding what you do, and you've taken your first step in organizing your life and preparing for your future!

Some items may simply be lost and need to be replaced; birth certificates, for example. You can obtain certified copies of birth certificates from the County Clerk of the state in which the birth took place for a fee, usually between $5.00 and $25.00. All states have websites that indicate how various official documents can be obtained and, usually, how much they cost. On the Internet, use Google or some other search engine; type in the name of the state and go to its main page.

With proper identification, insurers, banks, and other financial institutions will issue duplicate records and may or may not charge a fee.

Review all documents before filing them in your *Life File*. If you haven't looked at an old homeowners, car, or health insurance policy, now is the time. If you need a duplicate, call your broker and, at the same time, ask them to clearly explain the policy to you. If you're not sure about the terms of a policy or the terminology you are likely to hear in a conversation with a broker, read *Chapter 4, Insurance,* before you call. Take notes during your conversation with the agent and attach them to the policy in your *Life File*.

Updating and weeding out records will take some time and effort, but it may not be as loathsome as you think. Most insurance agents or bankers will be happy to answer your questions; you just have to make a start and follow through. Pace yourself, don't try to do everything in one day; there's no need to pile that kind of stress on yourself if you have time. Use your new shredder for obsolete documents, especially if any have your address, Social Security, telephone, or account numbers on them.

There is information and documentation that every household needs in an emergency. Some documents may be put away (does everyone know where?) and others may be around somewhere. In an emergency, "around somewhere" is as good as missing. To prepare for an emergency, even the youngest family member should know when and how to dial 911. All family members should carry identification and a copy of emergency telephone numbers (or they should be programmed into their cell phones) to contact parents, neighbors, or relatives and know where the emergency list of health care issues and medications is kept. We all hope we never have to use them, but what if we do? Are they there? Where?

You knock yourself out every day to assure that your family is well cared for and safe, yet most households don't have a simple list of emergency numbers, let alone information on medications or health issues. It's such a simple step. Some things we don't have time for; others we must make time for. This is one of them. Don't fail your family when they need you the most.

DISASTER PLAN

If you've never been in a fire, flood, earthquake, tornado, hurricane, or paralyzing snow or ice storm, count yourself lucky. Not knowing what to do and how to do it is life-threatening to you and your family. Being prepared with a **disaster plan** may be your only means of survival.

Plan your needs. If you must suddenly leave your home, all family members must know the best exit routes and where to meet; across the street or at some nearby landmark (not too close, but not too far for the young and old). A designated central contact person should be assigned; that is, someone who does not live in the home. In case family members are disbursed or not home during an emergency they can contact the main contact person for information.

Sit down and discuss emergency issues with your family if you haven't already done so. This is a safety measure; you are planning to keep your family safe, not frighten them. You may be surprised at how children can improve your plans.

It would be so much easier if we could schedule

life events the same way we schedule, say, lunch dates, but so far life has resisted this approach. Since we can't schedule our lives as neatly as we'd like, our best defense is a good offense. The U.S. Government Office of Homeland Security has an excellent Emergency Communication Plan reproduced in the *Appendix* (*Emergency Communication Plan*). File an up-to-date emergency plan in your **Life File** and give a copy to a relative or friend living nearby and, if possible, someone who lives in a different area or out of state. Also make a note on the emergency plan of who has a copy.

EMERGENCY PHONE NUMBERS

Every household should have an easily accessible list of emergency phone numbers (by or attached to the telephone, programmed into cellular phones, in the kitchen or near the front and rear doors are good places) and each family member should carry a copy with them. Give a copy to a relative or neighbor. Be sure the list is always up-to-date. (See *Emergency Telephone Numbers* in the *Appendix*.)

Keep an up-to-date list of all emergency numbers in your **Life File** and make a note on the list of who else, beside family members, has a copy.

FAMILY EMERGENCY INFORMATION

Adults. This should include information on each adult in the household: where they work, telephone contacts, and any medical information that would be important in an emergency. Give a copy to a relative or neighbor and keep one in your *Life File*. (See *Emergency Telephone Numbers* in the *Appendix*.)

Children. Same as adult information above, except school information replaces work for adults. Include the name of a specific person at school and their telephone number. Be sure the school contact understands that they are your main contact and make sure they know how to contact you at a moment's notice. Give a copy of this information to a relative or neighbor and keep one in your *Life File*. (See *Emergency Telephone Numbers* in the *Appendix*.)

Think of this information as a speed-dial to help and keep it simple: John Smith, Jr., has [xyz medical condition]; contact John Smith, Sr., at 111–111–1111 or Grace Smith at 222–222–2222.

On the up-to-date copy of emergency contacts and medical information in your *Life File*, also note the names, addresses, and phone numbers of the people you've given the list to and shred obsolete lists.

Let's pause here a moment. Look at your front door. When you go through it, do you know when you'll return? Really? When your husband, wife, or children leave your home, do you know when they'll return? Really? Will it be after an unforeseen side trip to a hospital? You may be the safest driver in the nation—but that doesn't mean a thing to someone running a red light. You are clearly smarter than average (you bought this book!); so let's see if you've covered all your bases.

In an accident or emergency, the clock starts ticking. When they arrive, the first place the police will look for information is in your purse or wallet. What will they find? Generally, your license with your name and address. Now what (tick, tick, tick)? The police have access to databases that will give your telephone number. If your children and husband or wife are at school or work, the police will probably get a recording and may or may not leave a message that will scare the daylights out of the one who receives it (tick, tick, tick). When will their message be received? Minutes, hours later?

You're getting the picture. Get up and go now, immediately, and make sure that everyone in your household has the information they need to contact each other and that emergency personnel need. *When Life Changes Forever* will be right here when you get back.

There is nothing more important for your family or loved ones. Do everything you can and whatever it takes to assure that they, and you, are able to reach each other in an emergency. This is not difficult—and you've probably put more thought into what you'll have for dinner. Get a small piece of paper, write your name and emergency contact information on it, and tape it to the back of your license. Do the same for everyone else. Or program "Mom (or Dad)-emergency" and the number(s) into your children's phones and the name of your husband or wife "[name of husband]-emergency" or "[name of wife]-emergency" into your phone. Use the form in the *Appendix* and add anything that you think is relevant on the back (allergies or medications).

None of us knows what will happen—what is beyond that door—but we can have some measure of control. It is life threatening and beyond imagination to try to deal with unexpected events that can overwhelm us in the blink of an eye. Unless someone else in the family or household has done this—it is up to you. *Do it. Now.*

SOCIAL SECURITY NUMBERS

Social Security numbers are nine-digit references issued by the Social Security Administration of the U.S. Government. It is unique to the person to whom it is issued and establishes, among other things, the amount of their Social Security and Medicare benefits. It is important that you safeguard this number and give it out only to those who absolutely need it for you to conduct your business. Don't carry the card in your purse or wallet; leave it home in your *Life File*. Your Social Security number is the access route to much of your financial and medical information. If it's lost, stolen, or otherwise compromised, report it immediately to your local Social Security office, or online at www.ssa.gov, and request a replacement. Any changes to your Social Security information must also be reported to the Social Security Administration; for example, if you change your name or address. Use their website or visit a local office.

The Social Security Administration sends an annual statement of benefits to each earner. If you haven't received yours, use their website to correct any out-of-date information and request one. Among the information on the statement are the benefits you have accumulated during your work history. A very good reason to carefully review this statement is to determine if there is any unexplained increase in these numbers. That is, for example, if suddenly two years ago the amount of your earned benefits increased and you can't think of a reason why that would happen (you didn't get a big raise or take on another job), it may mean that someone else is using your number. It is a federal offense to use someone else's Social Security number, but the person to whom the number was issued is the one who will ultimately pay the taxes if it goes undetected; and the Social Security Administration doesn't have the man- or computer-power to identify duplicates. If you suspect something like this, swing into action now. Contact your local Social Security office. You can make an inquiry at their website, but if your number is being misused, every hour counts; and it's going to take many hours to sort it out. The long-term affects for you are that if someone uses your benefits before you do, there may not be any benefits available when you expect (and are entitled) to receive them, and in the meantime, you will be paying someone else's taxes.

BIRTH CERTIFICATES

As mentioned, you can obtain certified copies from the County Clerk in the state in which the birth took place for a fee usually between $5.00 and $25.00. All states have websites that list the Clerk's name, address, and phone number and sometimes how much certificates cost.

Keep two copies for each family member in your *Life File*.

MARRIAGE CERTIFICATES

In the event of an incapacitating health problem or the death of a spouse, you will need copies of your marriage certificate to identify yourself to various banking institutions, government agencies (Veterans Administration), and state agencies (for property titles). You can obtain additional copies from the

County Clerk of the state in which the marriage took place. Go to that state's website for more information.

Keep at least three certified copies in your *Life File*.

DEATH CERTIFICATES

Obtain several (ten) copies of a **death certificate** from the mortician for storage in your *Life File*. They will be required to obtain benefits from government (veterans) agencies, at state authorities (to change deed titles), and at banking institutions. See the section on *Death and Coping* in *Chapter 5, Legal*.

ADOPTION RECORDS

Adoption records serve the same purpose as birth certificates but may not be obtained directly through most state websites. You may, however, contact the County Clerk in the state in which the adoption took place and request an application for duplicate records. The state website may provide information on how to apply.

Store in your *Life File*.

NATURALIZATION RECORDS

Naturalization records generally include Certificate

of Arrival, Records of Naturalization, Naturalization Depositions, and Oath of Allegiance.

File in your *Life File*.

PASSPORTS

Passports are for U.S. Immigration officials' use only when you enter or leave the United States or its territories, and they are now required for entry to the Bahamas, Bermuda, Canada, the Caribbean, and Central and South America. Some other countries also require a valid U.S. passport for entry. When not in use, keep your Passport in your *Life File*. When traveling out of the country, also bring a photocopy of your passport; use your passport for Immigration, leave it in the hotel safe, and use the photocopy elsewhere.

Passports are issued for ten years and cost about $100 (less if you're renewing). Applications for first-time users must be made in person. To find an application location in your area, go to http://travel.state.gov or call 1–877–487–2778. You can get an application at any U.S. passport agency, a federal or state courthouse, a U.S. post office authorized to accept passport applications, a travel agent, and at the State Department's website (an excellent source of information).

If your passport is nearing its expiration date, consider renewing; some countries will not permit entry if it is within 6 months of expiring. Any alteration of a passport will make it invalid. Return expired passports to the State Department or local facilities (as above) and it is required to renew it.

Always keep a photocopy of your passport in your *Life File*. When not in use, store your original in your *Life File*.

DIVORCE RECORDS

Should it become necessary to sort out any issues after a divorce, you will need copies of all divorce decrees. Keep them in your *Life File*.

ALIMONY RECORDS

These records define the amount of alimony paid or received. Should a dispute arise, you may need to produce them. Keep them in your *Life File*.

SCHOOL RECORDS

Keep current records for all family members in your *Life File*.

SAFE COMBINATIONS

Keep an up-to-date list in your *Life File* and shred any obsolete lists. If you have a bank safety deposit box, keep the keys in a clearly marked envelope in your *Life File*.

COMPUTER PASSWORDS

If you're an average American, you haven't changed your password in the last six months, if ever. Tsk, tsk. Passwords should be changed at least every three months. The problem is that if you're conscientious about changing your password regularly, you probably don't update your *Life File*. (Post-its are not a good idea.) Solution:

1. Create a document file (or "Word" file; as if you were beginning to write a letter) that contains only the date and new password. (In the new document, type "1/1/07 [today's date]" and "123xyz [your new password]").

2. Print the document.

3. File the printed copy in your *Life File*.

4. Exit out of the document file and click "No" when the computer asks if you want to save the file, which will delete it.

Don't forget to remove and shred the old copy in your *Life File*.

ORGANIZATION AND ASSOCIATION MEMBERSHIPS

Membership cards are much like credit cards when it comes to vulnerability to theft. Keep a complete list of your memberships (with the organization or association name, address, and phone number) in your *Life File*. It may be easier to simply make a photocopy of both sides of each card. If a card is lost or stolen, notify the organization to prevent unauthorized use. (See *Memberships List* in the *Appendix*.)

NEW CHAPTERS

With absolute certainty, it can be stated that life is uncertain. We are constantly turning a page on one phase of our lives and beginning new chapters. One chapter of life is marriage. It is not uncommon, however, for a couple's life experiences to take them individually along paths that are no longer as compatible as they once were. While separation and divorce end that chapter, some people turn the page and embrace new challenges. Others do not. And yet others have change thrust upon them. Whatever your situation, divorce and separation are definitely arenas that require professional assistance, but there are options to the traditional process that you might consider.

ARBITRATION

Arbitration during a divorce is when both spouses agree to settle matters before a court issues a final decree. Neither party may force the other to participate in the process. Arbitrators help a couple come to decisions on issues other than child custody and support. Proponents of this option say it is faster and less expensive than court proceedings; a divorce in court can take from months to years and cost many thousands of dollars per spouse. Most attorneys can provide the names of arbitrators who are usually divorce lawyers or retired judges.

With the help of attorneys, couples draw up contracts outlining how they want the process to work. They meet with the arbitrator, and at the end of the negotiation process the arbitrator files a decision with the court that becomes a binding court order. For all parties, the informal setting of an arbitrator's office is usually preferable to a public courtroom. One of its most appealing aspects is privacy: participants do not submit financial records or discuss sensitive issues in open court.

Arbitration can be difficult and rulings are generally binding but it makes sense if there are time-sensitive issues (such as rent or tuition) that a couple cannot resolve. It may also be appropriate for couples with complicated **assets**. In some states, arbitration decisions may be appealed.

MEDIATION

Mediation helps a couple negotiate a mutually

acceptable settlement. Mediators do not make recommendations to the court; they simply encourage and help couples to reach agreements on issues other than child custody and support. Mediation before a divorce goes to court will speed up the proceedings considerably. Qualifications of mediators vary widely; do your research. Your attorney will be able to suggest the names of mediators.

COLLABORATIVE DIVORCE

During the **collaborative divorce** process, a couple and their independent attorneys agree to settle divorce matters (other than child custody and support) out of court and all parties try to negotiate a settlement. The drawback is that if no agreement is reached, the process is ended and if the couple wants to try again, they must start over with different attorneys.

Other Assistance. When couples cannot agree on child supervision and welfare and these issues have not been settled by the court, a **parenting coordinator** can be hired. A parenting coordinator tries to reach an agreement, but if not, can make a (non-binding) recommendation to the court. Your attorney can suggest the names of parenting coordinators. Qualifications vary widely, check references.

Other Issues. It is getting more expensive to divorce, and an extra bite may be coming out of a couple's retirement plans. A little noticed federal law allows employers to charge employees for the legal and accounting costs of splitting up retirement plans. These costs can reach thousands of dollars, but you may be able to pay for them from your personal funds and/or negotiate sharing the expense with your ex-spouse or ex-spouse-to-be. Call the Benefits Officer to find out if there is a charge for this service and how these charges are handled.

Saying "I Do"—
The Second Time Around

If you find yourself contemplating a second union, read on. For those who do not wish to embark on the Love Boat again, there's enough life to embrace to fill many lifetimes.

When contemplating a mid- or late-life change of partner, there are many more considerations than there probably were the first time. You have worked for and accumulated assets, and as you look forward to a bright future, now is the time to take stock and prepare for and protect that future. It is not a time for doubt, and you certainly don't want to be in doubt about what's "yours," "mine," or "ours." And you don't have to be.

Good business practice requires a full audit of each business before any agreement to merge is signed. If potential business partners don't do the proper research, both parties could later be in serious legal trouble. A business consists of assets, liabilities, and goodwill. (Sounds like a marriage, doesn't it?)

When two people go into business together, legal documents are drawn up that define how the business will be operated, the responsibilities of each partner, what bank accounts will be established, how profits (and losses) will be managed, who will receive income (and how much), and many other details. These documents may also include a predetermined formula for how the business is valued or how one partner may buy out the other. Business partners can also purchase insurance to protect the surviving partner in the event of a death. This does not mean that they expect to fail; on the contrary, it means they are wise enough to place all their cards on the table in the beginning to protect each other.

A comparison between a business and a marriage may seem silly until you realize that a small business has a 40% chance of failing and marriages have a greater than 50% failure rate.

When it comes to the business of marriage, we are sometimes uncomfortable with the idea of asking for anything like an "audit," or even mustering the courage to discuss it. Get over it. Outstanding, unknown, or unresolved financial or personal issues that may not be compatible with your lifestyle and goals can have devastating affects. We've all heard unhappy stories about the consequences of being unprepared for remarriage. In this situation, what you don't know can hurt you.

PERSONAL REPORTS

While you will not be allowed to order another person's credit report from a credit-rating bureau, there are reputable private firms that specialize in obtaining credit and legal information on individuals, generally from databases to which private citizens do not have access. ChoiceTrust offers **personal reports** for a fee at www.choicetrust.com.

Don't feel that you're invading another person's privacy; the information you receive is public record—the company is just doing the leg work (or pushing computer keys) for you. If you feel uncomfortable, order a report on yourself and share it with your intended.

ADVISORS/PLANNERS

When contemplating marriage, it is important to know what each person brings to the table. We're human, and not everything we've done will be viewed as the smartest move in recorded history; buying a scenic lot on the San Andreas Fault or a seaside cottage on the Atlantic low-tide line may qualify as less-than-brilliant investments. Before the wedding bells chime is a good time to sort out less-well-thought-out actions, tidy up credit reports, and settle legal and other overdue issues.

Take charge of your life and plan now to secure your new future. To be effective, you need top-notch advisors.

Let's be clear about who these advisors are. Like a lot of old sayings, a "Jack of all trades is master of none" is just as true today. A professional is usually a member of a nationally recognized association (doctors and the American Medical Association, lawyers and the American Bar Association) and many must be licensed and are required to continually update their knowledge (Certified Public Accountants). A professional usually specializes in one area and many are also knowledgeable in related areas. A tax accountant/dog psychologist, however, is probably not the best choice to guide you through selling that beach house or scenic lot.

If you're unsure of which professional you need, the simplest approach is to categorize your issue. Use your *Life File* as a guide. Identify the overall category and then drill down to your issue. Let's say when organizing your *Life File*, you discover that federal, state, and local taxes have not been paid for five years. Clearly the overall category is Finance (taxes). It is also a Legal problem; so narrow your choices to tax attorneys. These are personal expenses, so again narrow your choices to personal tax attorneys. This is a good place to start.

Two notes: (1) Uncle Joe, a retired accountant, may be able to recommend a personal tax attorney, but he is not the professional you need. (2) Choose an independent person; that is, don't inherit an advisor. Your family attorney may be a valued friend of long-standing, but if he or she is not a personal tax attorney, move on; no hard feelings. Make sure the person giving advice has only your interests in mind and can make the correct recommendations. Spend time investigating their background and experience. Decisions you make and actions you take now will impact your future.

Having decided on an advisor or planner, make an appointment and think of your first meeting as a job interview: theirs. If they are answering the phone, looking at papers, or in any other way paying less-than-100% attention to you, politely excuse yourself and go on to the next candidate on your list. You are the paying customer and they should be perfectly clear on your concept of service. If they're not interested in your problem, why would you be interested in paying first-rate fees for second-rate service?

During their interview for your business, ask all the questions you need to, no matter how many times you rephrase the same question. "What does that mean?" is the simplest way to come to a basic understanding. You don't need to, and probably don't want to, become expert in their field but make sure you come away from the meeting with:

A. A general understanding of the scope of the problem. If it develops that it's more complex than you thought, make sure the advisor outlines the steps that must be taken. Take notes.

B. Ask how long the process will take and roughly how much it will cost (their hourly rates, filing fees, etc. Is there a price list?).

C. Ask about resources you can access to increase your understanding.

D. Is there anything you can do to reduce time and cost?

E. What documents are required?

F. And, finally, during their job interview, do not accept jargon or technical terms. Listen carefully, but if you don't understand, ask for an explanation and keep asking until you understand it. If you don't get it by the third explanation, the explanation is at fault, not you. Clear, concise language can be comprehended by nearly everyone. "Clean up your room" is clear and concise; "Rearrange your personal habitat to conform to parental expectations" is pretentious and unacceptable. You're paying for the visit, get your money's worth.

Every state has its own laws and you need experienced professionals to steer you through complicated issues. After you have selected your advisor, establish a working relationship. Long-term relationships are important for consistency and continuity. If you need more than one professional, remember that, especially during the planning stage, you don't want too many cooks stirring the pot.

Anticipate and be prepared. Make a detailed list of your assets or have relevant documents handy. Check your *Life File*, you should find everything you need there. You're working with people who charge by the hour or the quarter hour; don't spend one nanosecond rifling through irrelevant papers in a shopping bag. Time is *your* money.

Think of the "big picture." Before your appointment, write down what you are trying to accomplish. One of life's little ironies: never seek advice without knowing what advice you seek. But don't worry if you haven't the slightest notion of where you're headed or how to get there, that's your advisor's job. For most of us, life is not terribly complicated, but the road to achieving our goals can be. Your goal may be as simple as ensuring that your power of attorney is appropriate. If you're satisfied that your advisor has a clear understanding of what you want, probably the most you will have to contribute are information and documents and the advisor will handle the rest.

Prenuptial Agreements–Not Only for the Rich and Famous

Another way to assure your future is with a Prenuptial Agreement. Nobody likes a wet blanket, but reality happens on this two-way street. If you're at mid-life, you have 20–25 more earning years. Should anything unexpected occur, will that be enough time to replace assets and fund your retirement? If you decide against a "prenup," read this section anyway for steps you can both take to protect your future. Then let the festivities begin!

Prenuptial agreements are not a new idea, nor were they always for the wealthy or famous. Before the Married Women's Property Act of 1848, agreements were necessary for women in the United States because without one, all of a woman's property and assets were automatically transferred to her spouse. If they divorced or he died, she lost everything.

A prenup demonstrates your commitment to the union, and while it may seem less than romantic, it is also less than romantic to realize that a marriage is a legal contract with rights and responsibilities. If you have reached a stage of life that requires more guarantees than promises, a prenup is all the more important. (See also *Know Your Rights* below.)

A **prenuptial agreement** is created before marriage and usually centers on the rights and entitlements each person will have regarding marital assets but may contain whatever a couple wants (within the law). In the 1970s when they gained notoriety, some people went overboard and identified who was responsible for washing the dishes and who for drying. Mercifully, that pesky little hurdle to wedded bliss has been settled by affordable dishwashers.

By creating a prenuptial agreement, you and your fiancé can define and distinguish the separate property owned by each at the time of marriage, as well as its treatment during and after the marriage (does it become community property or remain separate?), and how you will treat earnings, inheritances, and gifts received before, during, or after the marriage.

A prenup is legally acknowledged in most states. They don't have to be filed with the court and can be set aside by a court in the case of fraud, duress (if one party was coerced into signing), failure to disclose (if relevant information was not revealed), unfairness, and if either party was not adequately represented by an attorney when it was executed. You will need an attorney to complete a prenuptial agreement to assure that what you want to accomplish is legal and appropriate and some states require that it be notarized. Select an attorney who specializes in matrimonial law.

The prenup is clear documentation of the assets each person brings to the marriage and is particularly important if one party has a lot fewer assets than the other. Standards for enforcing prenups vary from state to state, but essentially, four conditions must be met.

1. Each party must make a full and complete disclosure of their assets, liabilities, income, and other facts affecting their financial situation.

2. Each party must be represented by separate and independent counsel (or they may waive this condition, as long as that is clearly stated in the agreement).

3. The terms of a prenup must be fair at the time the agreement is made and in most states it must also be fair at the time of enforcement.

4. The court may set aside an agreement if enforcement would impoverish either party and create a risk that either party (or minor children) would require public assistance.

WHO NEEDS IT?

A prenup can safeguard assets, protect loved ones, keep a business in tact, or just streamline divorce proceedings. Many couples use them to prevent lengthy legal hassles if the marriage fails. Both parties and their respective families benefit from a clearly written understanding of rights and responsibilities; in particular, people with many more, or a lot fewer, assets than their intended, who have children from previous marriages, who own or are a partner in a business, or who have high earnings.

WHY DO I NEED IT?

Ask yourself the following questions. If you answer "yes" to any of them, you should consider a prenup.

Do you have children from a previous marriage?

In most states, a surviving spouse inherits one-third to one-half of an **estate**. A prenup will supersede the law and make sure your property is distributed as you wish.

Do you own a business or are you involved in a business or partnership?

A prenup can prevent a business from being cannibalized (broken up) or controlled by others. Check the partnership or shareholder's agreements. What are the provisions for the sale of a business or partnership, for sharing business responsibilities, and for the incapacitation or death of a partner?

Do each of you have significant assets or does one party have much more than the other?

A prenup may specify that premarital property is kept separate and include estate provisions tailored to meet special needs such as trusts. In case of a divorce, partners may wish to keep whatever property and/or investments (and the income from them) that they owned prior to the marriage. Some agreements also define spousal support (see below).

Are you concerned about your intended's debts?

A clearly written prenup can protect you from credit card and/or business liabilities before, during, and after the marriage.

Are you giving up a career or lucrative job?

An agreement may specify compensation for the loss of income if the marriage fails.

Other Issues. The prenup may specify how money will be spent during the marriage. If there is a business or other income-generating assets, an agreement can identify who will run the business, handle investments, receive income, and who will share and in what proportions funds from certain sources.

Consider addressing some of the following items.

Premarital assets. If it is agreed that any assets owned before the marriage are to be kept separate, you might consider creating a trust and transferring assets into the trust (see *Trusts* in *Chapter 5, Legal*).

Marital assets. A prenup may define how assets and earnings acquired (either jointly or separately) during the marriage will be handled. In many states, wealth accumulation after marriage becomes community property unless otherwise specified.

Retirement assets. Retirement plans are considered separate property in many states but a non-working spouse is entitled to a share. [Check the beneficiaries listed on pensions, IRAs, annuities, retirement accounts, and other plans (see *Chapter 2, Finance,* and *Chapter 6, Retirement*).] Before making any changes, check with a tax accountant about the tax implications.

Insurance and *Veterans benefits.* Many prenups require that both parties maintain life insurance policies that designate each other as beneficiaries for government benefits.

Estate planning. Prenups may include language regarding death benefits and provisions for the surviving spouse.

Inheritance. If inherited property or other assets are kept separate from marital property, they are generally not considered a part of the marital estate. This may be reinforced in the prenup.

Deeds and *titles.* All deeds and titles must be reviewed and updated before they are included in a prenuptial agreement.

Lifestyle and *support contributions.* The prenup may define the intentions of both parties regarding contributing to the lifestyle of the marriage (that is, non-financial contributions such as child rearing) or spousal financial support following the marriage.

Many agreements include specific language on spousal support and property division. Scaling clauses (that is, the amount of support offered may depend on the length of the marriage or some other criterion) are often included. A couple may agree, for example, that if the marriage only lasts a year or two, no spousal support will be involved and/or a financial settlement may be scaled over some number of years.

Wills, powers of attorney, and *trusts.* All wills, powers of attorney, and trusts must be reviewed for accuracy before they can be included in a prenup. All powers of attorney end with death, but trust terms, that may remain in effect for generations, should be reviewed and updated (see *Trusts, Chapter 5, Legal*).

Conflict resolution. Often in later marriages, competition arises among children of previous unions. A prenup may anticipate this issue and contain a conflict resolution clause.

Sunset clause. This type of clause indicates that the agreement will be reviewed, updated, or lapse on some date in the future.

And, finally, it is not uncommon to include language indicating that if certain events or behavior take place, the terms of the prenup are automatically changed.

If not a prenuptial agreement, what? A full-disclosure balance sheet of assets and liabilities. If you skip the prenup, you should both draw up a balance sheet to share with each other. It's a snapshot of your financial condition at that moment that shows what you'd have left if you paid all your debts. A negative net worth (owing more than you have) may be a sign of trouble and is surely a time when a personal report would be appropriate.

Being flexible and thoughtful are as important as a prenuptial agreement. Don't try to anticipate every situation, but remember that without a prenup, community property state laws may make decisions for you.

Looking Back to Move Forward

Unless you're trotting off to Las Vegas or some other haven for quickie marriages (and, incidentally, Las Vegas wedding chapels are no longer open twenty-four hours a day), the list of "to do's" may seem endless. For most people, the items "Change my will" and "Review my estate documents" never make the list. These items, if they are thought about at all, are left in the category of "things to do when we get back from the honeymoon."

They also fall into another category: high risk. Just

as we cannot go back and forth in time, we cannot un-ring wedding bells. Even if you're sure you'll deal with these matters later, you cannot deal with them after the ceremony in the same way as you can before. If, as you walk down the aisle as the new Mr. or Mrs., your spouse whispers, "I absolutely refuse to dry the dishes," you may be stunned into silence, but it's unlikely that you'll drive to a divorce lawyer's office rather than the reception. That's silly, of course, but there are much more serious issues, such as learning that your new spouse has children, enormous debts, or their previous spouse is the beneficiary of all their insurance, pensions, and financial holdings, that may initiate a long, costly divorce before the ink is dry on the marriage license.

Happiness is knowledge! When (not if) you've done your utmost to assure a bright, surprise-free future, you'll have already won the "Protect Myself" game. To play "Protect Myself," all you need are well-developed senses of fairness and responsibility, a little common sense and the initiative to do all the things that need to be done before you start down the aisle.

If you are marrying or remarrying, chances are you will change the terms of your will or at least execute a **codicil**. Each time you change your **will**, you have the option of rewriting it from scratch or just adding a supplement (or modifier) called a "codicil" by the legal profession.

WHEN LIFE CHANGES FOREVER

Before changing your marital status is also the time to review insurance policies (*Chapter 4*), trusts, powers of attorney, living wills, and health care directives (*Chapter 5*). When you change these documents, your attorney will add a sentence that states that the most current version supersedes all others. After death, insurance, annuities, retirement benefits, and other assets pass to the beneficiary(ies) listed. If you haven't updated the beneficiaries and your ex-husband is still a beneficiary of your life insurance, the proceeds will pass to him (who'll remember you with renewed fondness). Sometimes changing beneficiaries is overlooked or deferred ("I'll get to it later."). Not wise. As long as you're doing all this reviewing and updating, get it all done. You may forget it later, and if you've already discussed it with your intended, there is something slightly unsettling about not following through. Contact insurers and request change-of-beneficiary forms.

KNOW YOUR RIGHTS

Not all rights are created equal. Let's try to sort this out a little, beginning with defining assets. At its simplest level, an asset is anything that has resale value. Also referred to as property, an asset is not necessarily real estate that is also referred to as property.

PROPERTY RIGHTS

Overall, most personal property falls into one of four categories: **single-ownership**, **joint-ownership**, **community property,** or **trust assets**. Each category has its own ownership rights and within these categories, the rights to each are further refined. Types of assets are also a consideration; that is, one does not have the same right to a car (a non-income generating asset) as they do to an income-generating asset (seaside cottage rental). In addition, an important part of determining who owns an asset is how, when, where, and by whom it was acquired. Here are some generally accepted definitions.

Single-ownership. Usually a person owns property (or an asset) after having purchased it using their own income that was earned while residing in either a community property or non-community property state. They may use the property for pleasure or profit and dispose of it as they choose. They are responsible for all expenses and other charges, such as taxes. For the purposes of, say, a prenuptial agreement, separate property is defined as an asset owned prior to marriage.

Joint-ownership. When two or more people own an asset, their rights and responsibilities are determined by state law. Joint ownership implies at least two owners, though there are exceptions. Owners may be two individuals or they may be a married couple. Joint property is not the same as community property.

Community property. Nine U.S. states have community property laws: Arizona, California, Idaho, Louisiana, Nevada, New Mexico, Texas, Washington, and Wisconsin. In part, California, for example, defines community property as assets acquired by a husband and wife during the course of their marriage using income earned while they are residents of California or another community property state.

To test whether or not an asset is community property, it must be determined where the funds used to purchase the asset came from; that is, if the income used to buy the asset was earned in a community property state, the asset is considered community property.

The mix 'n match factor: a husband and wife may each (and together) own different types of assets (separate and/or community property) based on where and how the assets were acquired. State laws differ; check with a professional.

Trust property. Any asset transferred to a trust becomes the exclusive property of the trust (see *Chapter 5* and the *Glossary*).

There are many other rights you should be aware of; some include the following.

Qualified Domestic Relations Orders. If your new spouse was married before, their former spouse (sometimes politely referred to as "The Ex") may be eligible to receive a portion of their retirement benefits. The rights of The Ex, children, or other **dependents** (see the *Glossary* for more detail) to pension benefits are spelled out in divorce settlements and qualified domestic relations orders that are part of a legal judgment or divorce decree. Check these documents to determine what you are entitled to; if The Ex will receive some or all of your new spouse's retirement income or insurance benefits, you should know.

Pension and *Social Security benefits*. If your new spouse's Ex passed away before your new spouse retired, you may be eligible to receive pension benefits. And regardless of how often your new spouse was married before, you may qualify for survivor's benefits under the Social Security Act. (See the section on *Social Security* in *Chapter 6, Retirement*.)

Check the beneficiaries listed on all insurance policies, pension plans, wills, trusts, checking and savings accounts, and the agent(s) on powers of attorney.

Joint Assets. If you and your spouse have joint checking/savings accounts and either spouse passes away, all funds are frozen. There's no way to avoid this but there are ways to reduce its impact on your life exactly when you may need funds the most. Create an individual account that contains enough money for you to live on for three months without any income, which is about the length of time it will be before you receive insurance benefits. It doesn't take much time to establish such a bank account and it may save you a lot of anxiety. Although joint funds are frozen, some banks may allow you to withdraw enough money for daily expenses, but banks are notoriously conservative about how much you need to live on. Or they may flatly refuse without proper identification and documentation. You may also create a pay-on-death bank account that you can use immediately (see *Chapter 5, Legal*).

For each asset you own jointly (insurance policies, homes, businesses, or cars, for example), you have rights but not the same rights for all assets. As just mentioned with joint bank accounts, your access rights can be interrupted. It is important to know how your rights to assets can be impacted by the death or incapacitation of a joint owner.

Some of this may be a little surprising but it shouldn't be scary. The scary part is when ATM and credit cards are suddenly useless. There will always be unexpected events, but you can cut down on the number of surprises you'll have to deal with when you may be least able to cope.

Contact banks, insurers, and other lenders to determine the exact terms of each account. Make notes and file them in your *Life File*. If you find that you'll need a contingency plan (or the proverbial "Plan B"), get busy putting one together. If you need help accumulating an emergency fund, check out the *Budgets* section in *Chapter 6, Retirement.*

Debt. Knowing your rights is especially important regarding debt. If you and your spouse jointly purchased a home or car and have joint credit cards, unless you can pay off these loans or make payments for three months after the incapacitation or death of a co-owner, lenders can initiate a foreclosure process. If you have a three-month emergency reserve account, you'll be able to sustain yourself until you receive insurance or other benefits.

Don't set yourself up for nasty surprises; even if you're not in a crisis situation, think of how much more secure you'll feel knowing you have a firm grip on things. You *can* do this; all you need to get started is a pencil, paper, and a telephone, and the payoff is enormously comforting.

PLANNING YOUR NEW LIFE TOGETHER

Now that you've explored each other's finances and agreed, in principal at least, on how life will be managed, it's time to look to the future. Begin a discussion on any of the following topics and see where it leads.

Do we both have wills?

Are any powers of attorney up-to-date and appropriate?

Do we each have up-to-date living wills?

Do we each have a health care power of attorney?

Do we need more life insurance than we had before marriage?

Do either of us expect to inherit money or property and how will it be treated (jointly or separately; how will taxes be handled)?

Should any individual or joint assets be put in trust?

What financial projects do we want to accomplish and what will be the contribution of each?

What are our retirement plans?

How do we want our estate plans carried out?

How will joint assets be handled for the benefit of children and/or stepchildren?

Do either of us expect to support or educate dependents other than children or stepchildren? How will that be handled?

Do adult dependents need to be provided for in our estate plans? How will that be accomplished?

These questions are discussion topics; don't try to tackle them all at once and don't expect to have all the answers. But if you find you need to take action, get the wheels in motion.

No one likes unpleasant surprises, but if you don't have some idea about your future partner's feelings and thoughts on these matters, that's just what you may get. Make no mistake, marriage is a business and the time to talk about the "what-ifs" is when you are most optimistic; in the beginning before any change of status. No one knows what the future holds; it is important that each party have a clear understanding of what to expect.

MOVING/RELOCATION

Experts say that divorce and death are the most stressful events in life, but moving is in a close third place. Except for nomads, Americans are the most mobile population on earth; statistics show that on average we move every five years. Although these statistics may be influenced by September and June migrations of millions of students around the country, moving for any reason has its own set of stresses. There's lots of help, but most of it comes in the form of how a move is, or should be, handled, not the emotional and physical strain involved.

Does staying where you are and making home improvements make sense? Almost any home improvement will add value to your home and you may have to make them anyway before you can sell.

All buyers (should) get home inspections and if an inspector finds serious, or too many, problems, you're limiting the price you can ask, the number of buyers willing to take on a "fixer upper," and some buyers will insist that improvements be made before they sign on the dotted line.

Although renovation costs can be high, especially for structural changes or updating expensive spaces such as kitchens or baths, the cost of moving can be higher in economic and emotional terms.

Buying a new home involves sales commissions (2%-10% or more of the total price of the house), closing costs ($2,000-$10,000 or much more), mortgage payments, taxes, and a long laundry list of other incidentals (utilities, phones, water/sewage, cable, and shut-off/connections) before you get to moving costs. Talk to a local realtor to get an idea of these costs.

Check the CLUE (Comprehensive Loss Underwriting Exchange) report on the home you're thinking of buying. CLUE reports are obtained by the current owner or resident. Since the report contains all insurance claims made by the owner or resident, you should also consider the nature of the claims; that is, if claims were made for less-than-serious problems, the length of the report may be due more to the nature of the person making the claims than issues with the property. Reports can be obtained from ChoiceTrust at their website (www.

choicetrust.com) or through the mail for a small fee. Residents of some states are entitled to a limited number of free or reduced-fee reports. Before you sign on the dotted line, request a copy from your realtor. The report can help you evaluate some of the problems the house has had; and during your home inspection, give the report to the inspector who will then pay particular attention to the repairs to assure that they were done properly.

Moving companies distribute handy and useful checklists of what you should be doing eight weeks before the move date, six weeks before, and so on. But if you've lived in a home for five years or more, have a job, kids, pets, an attic, garage, basement, and telephones—think again. There are no rules, but think about how organized you are, how much time you actually have in a day, week, or month to devote to moving, how much time and effort each room will take to organize, and make your own decisions about how much preparation time you need. Fortunately, you've already created your *Life File* and needn't worry about important papers.

The savings you think you will achieve by packing your own belongings aren't necessarily so. Most movers will not guarantee the condition of an item they do not pack; others refuse to move prepackaged items altogether.

Moving is an expensive proposition, no doubt about it. For a small household, moving from

Boston to San Francisco can cost between $10,000 and $12,000, and every mile increases the cost. And, yes, you do want the insurance. The upsides are that professional movers arrive like a swarm of locust, pack everything down to the last box of tissues in less than a day or two, load it on a truck, and are gone; and you don't have to live with wall-to-wall boxes (moving is irritating enough without adding to it). If you've given the movers lots of labels to slap on the boxes as they move from room to room, the boxes will magically appear in the correct rooms of your new home.

Holding a garage or yard sale entails time, muscle, and, in some cities, a permit. Are the few dollars you may (or may not) make really worth it? Consider donating as much as possible to worthy charities. You may request donation letters that will allow you to write off the fair market value of the goods at tax time.

Sellers usually deliver a house in "broom clean" condition. The truth is that often means their possessions have been removed. Great for the seller, but it may not be your idea of clean. Send someone ahead or hire a cleaning service before the moving truck arrives, especially if heavy-duty cleaning (walls and carpets) is involved.

Negotiate a few days at your old home after the closing date to give yourself time to get the new place in shape. It may cost some rent dollars but will give you a much better shot at the fresh start you want.

Whether you're coming, going, or staying, here are some home maintenance projects that will safeguard your home's long-term health.

Roof	Check for leaks around vents, skylights, and chimneys.
Attic	In the spring, open vents for ventilation; close in the fall to conserve heat. Check for roof leaks (water stains) and critters.
Gutters	Be sure gutters drain away from the house. Clean annually. If you have an enthusiastic leaf-dropper tree nearby, consider covering gutters with screens.
Paint/Siding	Look for and repair cracks, chips, and holes.
Windows/ Doors	Make sure all seals are airtight; repair as needed. Seventy percent of your heating/cooling dollars ooze through these gaps.
Fireplaces	Absolutely have all fireplaces professionally cleaned annually; a soot-filled chimney is a serious fire hazard. Make sure the damper closes securely to reduce heating/cooling loss.

Heating/ Cooling Systems	Service in the spring (cooling) and fall (heating). Make sure inside vents are clean and unblocked.
Air Filters	Clean or replace filters often (don't forget dryers and stove hoods).

Refrigerator	Door seals should be airtight and the door should close securely. Place a dollar bill on the doorframe and close the door; if you can easily remove the bill, the seal should be replaced because there are lots of energy dollars slipping by that old seal. Vacuum or dust exterior coils twice a year.
Faucets/Taps	You'd be surprised at how quickly a dripping tap can fill a gallon pot. Repair leaks inside and out.
Basements	Check walls for dampness or leaks; repair as necessary.
Safety Equipment	Check all smoke and gas detectors; make sure batteries are operating. Do you have the correct fire extinguishers for kitchen and elsewhere (there is a difference)?

Try to do all inspections routinely in the fall and spring (perhaps when resetting clocks). Make it easy on yourself; change all filters and batteries at the same time; batteries are cheap, you're safety is not.

Some of these projects we can do ourselves, others not. If you need a contractor:

* Ask for recommendations at your local hardware or home improvement store; contractors practically live there. Ask friends and neighbors who will give you an honest assessment of a contractor's work quality.

* *Always,* always, *always* check references. (Reference*s:* plural.)

* Make sure the contractor is licensed and insured.

* Check with the local Better Business Bureau before hiring anyone.

* Always discuss expectations with a contractor to be sure they understand what you want to achieve.

* Always get a written estimate or contract.

* Never allow contractors to employ undocumented workers to perform your repairs or construction; it is against the law, and if an accident happens you are risking a great deal more than the contract cost. Citizenship is not required to file a lawsuit.

CHAPTER 2: *Finance*

VALUE VS. COST: IMPROVE YOUR ODDS & YOUR FUTURE

"Rich," "comfortable," "well off," and other terms that describe wealth are subjective. We all have our own idea of how much money we need to live happily; anything more is gravy and not necessary for our well being. It's fun to dream of winning a huge lottery, but what are the odds? There's a very large segment of the population that would like to reach a level of wealth that meets their needs and enables them to live without worrying day after day about the next mortgage or car payment.

This chapter is not an economics lesson. Money is a tool, a means to an end and that's all. For most of us, that end or goal is to live as comfortably and as worry free as possible now and in the future. If you're constantly dreading the mail or debate every time you want to buy some small personal item, as opposed to not buying it and paying bills, you need to take positive action now.

According to some experts, women make 94%

of the decisions for home furnishings, 92% for holiday buying, 91% for home buying, 89% for new bank accounts, and 88% for medical care. (And you thought you weren't a factor in a U.S. economy of trillions of dollars!) On the other hand, only 12% of women take responsibility for planning and investing their money. Women also have a 70% chance of being ultimately responsible for their own financial strength and an 80% chance of being responsible for another person's.

We often hear the term "financial health," but "health" implies breathing and heartbeats that are passive and involuntary. Financial "strength" is more descriptive as it implies empowerment and self-control, exactly what you want to accomplish.

YOUR LIFE FILE

There's a long list of items in the Finance folder; let's look at the most common first.

ASSET LIST

When you buy a refrigerator, you assume it will work for the next thirty years. But six months later your shiny new appliance is leaking, the wiring has shorted out, or the crisper is a balmy 78°. When you call the seller, they will ask for the sales slip and warranty information. Your options are to produce the paperwork, have it repaired yourself (up to manufacturer's standards to protect the warranty), or buy a new one. If you're using your *Life File*, you're golden; all the paperwork (sales receipts and warranties) is at your fingertips.

A refrigerator is an asset that should be included on your asset list. If the leak damaged flooring, walls, or household wiring, and needs to be included on an insurance claim, your asset list will provide the information that the insurance company will require. This list shouldn't be "1 refrigerator, 4 clocks, and 3 tables," but rather a detailed list of items that includes an accurate description of each item, sales prices, purchase dates, and any other relevant information. For one-of-a-kind items (pictures, collectibles, or antiques) take a picture of each and keep them with the Asset List in your *Life File*. Have rare or unique items appraised (an insurer may insist on this before it will insure an item) and insure them separately.

Keep any appraisals in your *Life File* attached to the insurance policy. As you update this list, shred the old one. (See the sample form in the *appendix*).

AUTOMOBILE RECORDS

Because the records for automobiles cross several *Life File* categories, you might consider using a separate folder for each vehicle and keeping an overall list of multiple vehicles.

A copy of the title or "pink slip" should be kept in the *Legal* folder.

Insurance policies should be kept in the *Insurance* folder. Before you file them, check that they are current and appropriate to your needs. If you think it's appropriate, and even if you don't, check with your insurance broker to be sure that you are neither overinsured nor underinsured.

The registration and proof of insurance should be kept in the vehicle and a copy of each should be filed in the **Life File** *Legal* folder.

Check warrantee expiration dates and file in the *Insurance* folder or if they have expired, shred them.

Maintenance records should be kept in the *Insurance* folder.

An extra set of keys (or access codes) should be kept in a marked envelope in the *Insurance* folder (or the *Family* folder; it's your **Life File**, make your own rules).

BANK ACCOUNTS

Keep a complete and up-to-date list of all bank, credit union, and brokerage accounts in the *Finance* folder of your **Life File** and shred all obsolete lists.

Many people have automatic deposits (for example, paychecks or Social Security benefit checks) or withdrawals (bill paying) from their checking accounts. Without specific information, these automated transactions are difficult and time consuming to trace. Keep an up-to-date list in the *Finance* folder of your **Life File**. The list should contain the name of the company making the withdrawal, their telephone number, address, and the amount of the withdrawal. Bank statements often have coded identifiers of automatic withdrawals that may include an abbreviated company name and telephone number. For example, "SMT5428005551234" may identify the Save My Time company whose phone number is 800–555–1234. If not, contact your bank to get the exact reference and note it on your list.

Always select an interest-bearing checking account. When you're not using it, the money is working for you earning interest.

Brokerage houses offer checking but not saving accounts. Since the purpose of a brokerage account, with optional checking, is attached to trading stocks, bonds, and other financial instruments, their requirements regarding minimum balances are slightly more stringent than those of commercial banks.

ATM cards. There are two kinds of ATM cards. One is signature-based, usually with a VISA or MasterCard logo that looks like a credit card but has no credit available. The other is based on a Personal Identification Number (PIN). The difference between the two is how each transaction is handled by the bank. With the signature type you sign for your purchase and the money is deducted from your checking account in two or three days. Always use the signature (or "credit") option when swiping; using the credit option usually does not involve a transaction fee. With the PIN type, the amount of your transaction is immediately deducted from your checking or savings account and some banks (and probably, soon, most banks will) charge for each PIN transaction.

Using another bank's ATM machine creates two charges: one for using the ATM machine and one from your bank. These charges can be as high as $10 per withdrawal (amounting to about $4 billion a year windfall for banks). Go to your bank's website to find the locations of their ATMs and use them.

Keep the last 12 bank statements in your *Life File* and shred old ones. If, for any reason, you need statements from earlier dates, they can be ordered from the bank for a fee.

BANKRUPTCY

Let's talk about how to avoid this situation and its consequences before tackling the 800-pound gorilla.

Each situation is different, but some general assumptions can be made. If your annual income is, say, $50,000 and your debts are $45,000, you are already over the edge and in freefall and **bankruptcy** is a real possibility. A rule of thumb is that if rent or mortgage and debt payments total much more than 58% or 60% of your total income, you're on shaky financial ground. Here, "debt" means mortgages, car or other loans, but not credit card debt. For an instant analysis of your finances, see the *Bankruptcy: Two-Minute Warning* form in the *Appendix*.

To avoid bankruptcy, you can rob Peter to pay Paul, but this strategy has its limits and it's not the wisest policy if only from the standpoint of the number it will do on your nerves. Sooner or later this strategy will catch up with you.

Statistics indicate that bankruptcy among middle-aged people can be attributed to job loss and sky-rocketing medical costs. In addition, because people are living longer, middle-aged Americans are now eight times more likely to have a living parent as did previous generations. This so-called "sandwich" generation is often responsible for both their children and their parents. When people wait until their thirties to begin families, tuition bills and other expenses come later in life when most people are looking forward to retirement.

Middle-aged bankruptcy filers, many of whom are homeowners, often try to pay credit card debt using home equity loans (see *Use Your Home Equity Wisely* below). This is a very slippery slope. The homeowner may clear their credit card debt but now has a high-interest loan to pay using their home as collateral; if they default on the loan, they could lose everything.

Homesteading your residence, if you haven't already done so and live in a Homestead-acceptable state, is a must (see *Chapter 4, Insurance*).

One of the most common mistakes bankruptcy filers make is to use their retirement funds to satisfy personal debt. The mistake is that retirement plans are generally protected by the court; that is, in a bankruptcy, retirement funds will not be included among your assets.

And finally, people stall, often for years, while contemplating or trying alternate strategies. This may be the worst practice of all as interest accumulates while they fall further and further behind.

The smartest policy is to figure out what you can do about the situation before bankruptcy looms large on your horizon and get busy doing it.

Some people advocate creating a budget and writing down every dime you spend. That's okay for them, but most of us don't have the willpower or time for that. Creating a budget shouldn't be an exercise in penance and you *can* develop the discipline to follow one. There are many ways to cut back on spending; some painless and others involve a little thought and preparation. You just need the honesty to create a reasonable budget that you can live with, the discipline to pass up impulse spending, and the desire to turn things around. (See *Budgets* in *Chapter 6*.) *It can be done.* You can find samples of budget forms on the Internet, at bookstores, and there are organizations that can help. Ask your bank or credit union for help. It's in their interest for you to remain solvent, or ask the local bankruptcy court for information.

Very sobering. If you're thinking about filing for bankruptcy, you must know what will be included among your assets. Some items are exempt (will not be included in the process), such as pension plans or, in most states, a residence, but each state has its own statutes. Well before you file an application, think very, very long and hard about this process and get professional advice.

In a nutshell, bankruptcy is the development of a plan that allows a debtor to resolve their debts either through the division of assets or a managed program of repayment. The process is supervised by trustees of the bankruptcy court. The most common form of bankruptcy, called "Liquidation" (or "Chapter 7"), is when a court trustee collects all the non-exempt property (that will be included in the process) of the debtor, sells it, and distributes the proceeds to creditors. Another form, called "Reorganization" ("Chapter 13"), is for people who want to pay off their debts over three to five years. Reorganization appeals to people with non-exempt property or assets that they want to keep and is only available to people with enough predictable income to cover reasonable living expenses with enough left over to repay their debts. Other forms of bankruptcy allow business owners to stay in business and use the revenue to pay creditors.

Bankruptcy may be voluntary or involuntary: you may initiate the application (voluntary) or creditors may begin the process (involuntary). Debtors may not transfer property or assets (to any other person or entity) for three years before filing a bankruptcy application.

Some courts require debtors to take part in credit counseling sessions during the six months prior to filing a bankruptcy application and/or complete a financial education course between the time of filing the application and when it is approved by the court. During these sessions, credit counselors help analyze spending habits, work out budgets, and may negotiate with creditors to create a manageable repayment program.

The consequences of declaring bankruptcy will impact your future in some unexpected ways: some companies and government and civil agencies refuse to hire people who have declared bankruptcy; it will be reflected on your credit report for at least seven years, and during that time most lenders will not extend credit; creditors may file liens on your property or estate that will take a long time to resolve; and the Internal Revenue Service will lead the parade to your doorstep and they *will* get their cut first. Don't expect the state or government to pick up the tab; the days of "walking away" from credit card debt are over. A recent federal law declares that 25% of credit card debt or $10,000 (whichever is greater) must be repaid.

The best way to avoid this unhappy situation is to take command of your life now. *You can do this.* It really doesn't take that much time or effort to create a budget, and getting finances in hand will be a lot more satisfactory than bankruptcy. But if you feel that bankruptcy is your only option (and it usually is not), seek professional advice.

Lenders claim that they can collect all your debts into one basket, lower the monthly payment, and get you out of debt sooner than you can yourself. Before you decide on this option, investigate more than one offer. Lenders are in business for one reason: to make money. No matter how they try to portray themselves as your Dutch uncle, their objective is making money, and one way or another they will. If you've zeroed in on two or three offers, take the paperwork to a lawyer or (tax) accountant and have the offers analyzed. This will involve a charge for the visit but in the long run may save more than your money. If part of the lenders' deal is using your home(s) and car(s) as collateral, be very wary. During your visit with the attorney or accountant, they may be able to suggest alternate plans. Ask them.

A list of agencies approved by the U.S. Trustee Program can be found at www.usdoj.gov/ust. This is a very worthwhile website to check out.

BUDGETS

A budget is nothing more than an honest assessment of your financial strength. Don't groan; the idea that once you create a budget you're locked in to it is nonsense. A budget is a snapshot of where you are financially at the moment, where your money is going, and how much you have for discretionary (extra) spending. That's it. End of story.

If you decide to create a daily budget, it should be flexible. Unless you want to account for every penny, don't create something you can't live with or you'll very soon become discouraged and skip the whole thing.

Creating a budget requires some thought, time, a long list, and honesty. If you're going to fudge the numbers, forget it. The bright side is that in the end you'll know how much you're spending and see places where you can make changes. Take a look at the *Budgeting* section in *Chapter 6*. Fill in the generic form with rough guesses and then look for places where you can make cuts. You *can* make things happen when you have an overview, set goals, and take charge.

CREDIT CARDS

Whether you have a *Life File* or not, go now, directly to the nearest copier and make a copy of both sides of every credit card you have. Without these copies or the cards (or the up-to-date list in your *Life File*), if you need to contact these lenders, it will be difficult and time-consuming to find their contact information to report lost or stolen cards. In the meantime, anyone who finds (or took) them will have plenty of time to use them.

Why do casinos use colorful disks roughly the size of half dollars? Because very soon after beginning to play with them, if we think of them at all, we think of them as toys, not money. There are whole areas of science devoted to tricking your brain into thinking something is not what it really is. Advertisers are masters at tricking you into thinking that you're getting something for nothing or that your life will be immeasurably improved by the use of their product. The truth is, whether or not the product improves your life or is a useless annoyance, eventually we pay for everything.

Another science is value assessment: placing a value on everything. Not everything has a value. Costs are money, but value is often emotional.

What is the cost/value of a tire? Its value is that your car won't work without it. If you need to food shop, the tire is necessary and has a real value; you won't have food without the tire. The cost is that if the tire is missing or punctured, it will cost to replace or repair it.

Credit cards work on the same principals. Issuers hope that you will cave in to every advertisement to add cost after cost and sincerely hope you know nothing about value assessment. Signing your name to a credit card sales slip commits you to a lot more than a purchase: you are committing your future income (cost) and defining your future lifestyle (value).

To squeeze ever more money from customers, lenders have become extraordinarily creative at adding charges; it's how they make most of their money. Daily charges, variable or flat monthly service fees, per transaction charges, and fees for late payments, annual use, speaking with a representative, copies of transactions, dormancy (not using an account), closing an account, monthly maintenance (not to be confused with a regular monthly fee, although since everything is in the computer, how much and what maintenance is required is anyone's guess), and anything else they can dream up to add costs, not value. The average American pays between $600 and $1,000 per year for bank service fees.

Why is your minimum monthly payment 2%-5% of the total balance? The simple answer is it looks good (lender public relations), and for a very long time your monthly payments are only applied to the interest (not the principal). Free money for banks and lenders. It has been reported that these payment percentages are expected to double in the near future; if your monthly payment is $200, expect it to increase to $400. Paying the minimum balance locks you in to monthly payments for the next 20 or 30 years if you stop charging today. Great for the credit card issuer but not so great for you.

Let's look at some hard numbers.

Total credit card balance: $2,000
Minimum payment: 2%
Annual interest rate: 18%
Total months to repay (if you stop charging today and only make the minimum payment): 94 months (that's almost *8 years*)
Total interest you'll pay: $1,724 (in addition to the original $2,000).

An 18% interest rate is rare. Let's look at the norm.

Total credit card balance: $2,000
Minimum payment: 3%
Annual interest rate: 24%
Total months to repay (if you stop charging today and only make the minimum payment): 56 months (*almost 5 years*)
Total interest you'll pay: $1,329 (in addition to the original $2,000).
To calculate your credit card interest, see *http://finance.yahoo.com/personal-finance,* at Calculators, go to "How long will it tak to pay off my credit cards?"

Paying the suggested monthly amount is just plain foolish if you can afford to pay more. For a very long time none of your payment will be applied to the principal. Send a check for the monthly payment and a separate check to be applied to the principal. The second check doesn't have to be much but mark it "Principal Only" on the memo line. The more of the principal you can pay off, the less time it will take to pay off the entire amount and the less interest you will pay. If you can afford to pay, say, $50 on a credit card that requires a monthly payment of $20 ($20 for the minimum payment and $30 on principal only), you will substantially reduce the time it takes to pay off the balance.

Any financial planner worth their salt recommends minimizing the number of credit cards you carry (to 2), getting the best interest rates available, and avoiding any card with an annual fee. It's excellent advice.

If you haven't cut up your cards by now, let's look at some of those creative charges that have nothing to do with value.

Daily interest. Every day when you wake up, somewhere a computer goes "ka-ching" as it adds a charge to your balance. Not much value to you.

Late payment fees. Some late payments are fixed, others depend on your balance, and some are scaled. A fixed fee is a stable amount (say $15-$35) charged for each late payment. Balance-based fees depend on your monthly balance and vary each month (if your balance is, say, $500 and the late payment is 2% of the balance, the late payment will be $10). A scaled fee is based on an increasing interest rate per late payment. For example, the first late payment fee may be calculated based on 5 points above the lender's usual interest rate. If the lender usually charges 24% interest, the first late fee would be calculated at 29%. The second late payment fee may be calculated at 15 points above the usual interest rate (or 39%), and the third late fee may be based on 25 points above the usual rate (or 49%). Very serious money (that has no value to you) if your balance is $15,000 and you've missed two payment dates.

Avoid late payments. If last month's payment was late, this month's minimum payment will be applied to the late fee first, interest second, and principal last. If the minimum payment is, say $20, and the late fee was $25, you really haven't paid anything on your bill; in fact, you've added to it. The credit card company got (a free) $20: $20 is applied to the $25 late fee, nothing on the interest or principal, and $5 is added to your balance.

Imbedded in the fine print of some credit card contracts is something called a "universal default" clause. This allows the issuer to make routine checks of your account and if they find that you're late making payments to them, or anyone else (other credit cards, car loans, or mortgages), they can raise your interest rate without notice. It has recently been reported that Congress is investigating universal default clauses and their possible elimination. Time will tell.

Turn it around. The sooner you make the payment, the better; when you get the bill, pay it. No late charges.

Cash advances. Ugly. Cash advances are loans, not revolving credit. Revolving credit means that credit card balances, no matter how much they go up or down (revolve), are based on the repayment terms outlined in the contract you originally signed to get the card. Cash advances are personal loans with higher interest rates. Ka-ching, another money outlay that has no value to you but most certainly has a cost.

But for lenders, it gets even better. Cash advances are automatically shuffled to the bottom of the deck and you are required to settle up on all purchases (revolving charges), as well as monthly fees, late charges, and all other related interest, before the computer will deal with cash advances. This means that cash advances are sitting out there acquiring interest at a higher rate than for your revolving charge items waiting for you to repay everything else. By the time you get to them, the total accumulated interest will be substantial.

Willy-nilly credit card spending is dangerous. Before even considering the price of an item, think about its value. Charging $5.00 worth of Cheetos at a grocery store and paying 25% interest on them for a year or two or three, is…well, bananas. Can you wait and buy an item later for cash and pay no interest at all?

You probably can't stop the avalanche of "preapproved" (that never are) credit card solicitations, but a good way to slow it down is to send them all back the same way they arrived: blank. After a company spends about $7.00 to print and send it, it gets their goat if they also have to pay return postage and throw out their own trash. Or think: shredder (but use scissors on plastic items).

Credit card debt analysis companies advertise that they can reduce your debt, and no doubt some can, if they are reputable. Disreputable companies will take your check and forget your name before it's deposited. Do your homework; check references and with the local Better Business Bureau.

Joint credit cards. If your signature is on a joint credit card account, you are responsible for the balance even if you've never used it.

If you don't want to contribute to the estimated $15 billion that banks make on service charges, look for a truly free checking or ATM card. Check with local banks or credit unions (see www.creditunion. coop for a credit union in your area).

Recently, a bank offered its customers a 23-point interest rate reduction (from 28% to 5%) if they would use automatic bill paying. (Where do I sign?) Call your bank to find out if they offer any interest rate reduction for this option.

Keep the last 12 statements in your *Life File*.

CREDIT BUREAUS/CREDIT SCORES

Under the Fair Credit Reporting Act, every American is entitled to a free annual credit report. To obtain yours,

Visit www.annualcreditreport.com ; or
Call toll-free: 1–877–322–8228
The website contains an application form. Fill it out online, or print and complete it, and mail to:
Annual Credit Report Request Service
P.O. Box 105283
Atlanta, GA 30348–5281

The Federal Trade Commission reports: "An amendment to the Fair Credit Reporting Act requires each of the nationwide consumer reporting companies—Equifax, Experian, and TransUnion— to provide you with a free copy of your credit report, at your request, once every 12 months. The three companies have set up one central website, toll-free telephone number, and mailing address (above) through which you can order your free credit report. The Federal Trade Commission, the nation's consumer protection agency, wants you to know that if you want to order your free annual credit report online, there is only one authorized website: www. annualcreditreport.com. Many other websites claim to offer 'free credit reports,' 'free credit scores,' or 'free credit monitoring.' But be careful. These sites are not part of the official annual free credit report program."

The best reason to get an annual report is to make sure that someone isn't opening credit card accounts under your name (or trying to) or making purchases on your cards.

MyMoney.gov website is an excellent resource.

Credit scores, also called FICO scores, are based on information and calculations generated by the Fair Isaac Corporation (FICO) in California. Your score is based on many bits of data and range between 450 and 850. It is based on your past use of credit, how many revolving charge accounts you have and how you have handled them, as well as other odd bits (having too few credit cards is one). Surveys have repeatedly found that 20% of the information on credit reports is incorrect. "No matter," say banks and lenders, "clean up your act or you won't get one cent from us."

While most of us routinely accept incompetent service at the mall or over the phone because it doesn't cost much more than a little time, when incompetence is costing us real dollars, we should think of it in different terms: what is the value to me? How much is someone's incompetence taking away from my life today (in real, hard-earned cash), and how will their incompetence impact my future?

If they're so sloppy, why do banks and lenders bother with them? Because they're the only game in town; no one else will do the leg work, and lenders don't care because they view it as your responsibility to straighten it out and oversee your own destiny.

Well, fine. Let's beat them at their own game. They are:

TransUnion, 1–800–888–4213
P. O. Box 1000, Chester, PA 19022
www.transunion.com

Experian, 1–888–397–3742
P. O. Box 2002, Allen, TX 75002
www.experian.com

Equifax, 1–888–685–1111
P. O. Box 740241, Atlanta, GA 30374
www.equifax.com

Request your free annual report from each bureau. This is not overkill or redundant; each bureau may have a different score for you. When you receive them, you will also receive a brochure that explains their report. Read it carefully and review each item.

Don't worry if you don't understand the reports and/or the explanations (you're not alone), call the reporting bureaus and speak to a representative.

Cautions: when requesting a report online from these bureaus, they may require that you sign an agreement for about $15.00 a month that allows you to check your credit frequently. They may offer the first month free and clearly state that they will charge you $15.00 a month until you cancel. If you don't cancel at the end of the trial period, they'll get lots of $15.00 charges from your checking account until you do. Some banks also offer a "free" credit report for $1.00. Go figure. You're entitled to an absolutely fee report once every 12 months.

The next step is to correct mistakes. Credit bureaus, realizing the inferior quality of their product, include several forms for the purpose. Complete them as accurately as you can and submit them to the credit bureau.

A high credit rating score has rewards. People with scores greater than 760 are offered the best interest rates on mortgages or other loans and insurance premiums. For a quick comparison, FICO offers the following table. In real terms, the difference between a credit score of 500 and one of 760 is $740 a month. While FICO doesn't determine interest rates, it certainly influences the annual percentage rate you'll be offered.

30-year Home Equity Loan			
FICO Score	Annual Percent	Monthly Payment	Difference
500-579	9.418%	$2,505	$193
580-619	8.526%	$2,312	$299
620-659	7.086%	$2,013	$161
660-699	6.276%	$1,852	$55
700-759	5.992%	$1,797	$42
760-850	5.770%	$1,755	

The column labeled "Difference" has been added to display two things: (1) clearly, there are a great many people in the 580–619 score range because if they weren't the largest population of all the score groups, they wouldn't be hammered as badly as they are; and (2) if you haven't cleaned up your credit score to achieve at least 660, you're losing a significant amount of money every day.

Clean up your credit score and then go to every credit card company, banker, broker, insurer, and anyone else you owe money to and ask them to review your new credit score and ask for interest rate reductions.

Smart borrowers land the best interest rates. Be a smart borrower: pay bills on time. A lender that sees a pattern of late payments will probably (almost assuredly) raise the interest rate they are willing to offer you. Some lenders consider three consecutive missed payments an indication that the balance will never be repaid and will not extend credit or may begin legal proceedings.

Reduce credit card balances: if you use a high percentage of the available credit (50% or more), it is assumed that you're spending beyond your means and will have trouble making payments, which lowers your score. But don't feel that you're being singled out; lenders are very democratic and so anxious to demand high rates that even if you have a very high score, using more than 20% of your available credit will negatively affect your credit score. "Maxing out" credit cards is never, ever a good idea; if you have any cards that are maxed, cut them up and get them paid off as quickly as possible.

Limit credit applications to four or less in a six-month period. Each time you apply for credit, lenders check your credit rating and too many inquiries also lowers your score. All inquiries within a 45-day period are considered one inquiry; the theory is that you are shopping for an item and have gone to several places that all checked your credit.

And, finally, build a track record. With no credit you have no credit score and lenders will probably refuse any loan or credit card application. FICO does not distinguish between creditors who carry a balance and those who do not. It knows you have a credit card but, after that, really only cares about late or missed payments. So don't be late or miss payments. Or carry only a very small balance and make those payments promptly. If you decide to get a credit card and use it only for very small purchases to build your credit rating, make sure it is not one that charges an annual fee. The American Consumer Credit Counseling (www.consumercredit.com or 1–800–769–3571) is an excellent resource.

CREDIT UNIONS

Credit unions are essentially private banks usually associated with large companies. Credit union and bank interest rates are fairly competitive with credit unions offering slightly better (lower) lending rates. Membership in company credit unions is usually restricted to employees, but private credit unions welcome everyone. The appeal of (employee) credit unions is convenience and favorable interest rates. Many private credit unions servicing local areas offer similar benefits.

Keep the last 12 credit union statements in your *Life File* and shred old statements.

IDENTITY THEFT

Identity theft is a nasty business that you may not know about until it has gone on for months. If you're on the East Coast and the thieves are on the West

Coast using your identity to open credit card accounts and charge up a storm, it could be several months before notices of unpaid bills begin to arrive in your mail. In the meantime, however, late and missed payments are being noted on your credit report.

The key here is your Social Security number. Let's repeat: The key is your Social Security number. Have you noticed the important word in that sentence: *your*. If you give your Social Security to a-n-y-o-n-e you are welcoming the spider into your parlor. Just do not do it. No reputable company will ask for it over the phone and all disreputable people will. Do not write it on your checks; do not give it to salespeople in person and never on the phone; and do not carry it in your wallet.

But if you've taken every precaution and are still a victim, you must swing into action immediately.

1. Contact the fraud departments of the three major credit reporting bureaus:

   TransUnion, 1–888–680–7289
   P. O. Box 6790, Fullerton, CA 92834

   Experian, 1–888–397–3742
   P. O. Box 2002, Allen, TX 75013

   Equifax, 1–800–525–6285
   P. O. Box 740256, Atlanta, GA 30374

Ask that a "fraud alert" be placed on your file. This indicates to any company checking your credit that your information has been compromised and they must contact you personally before authorizing any credit.

As the victim of fraud, you are entitled to a free credit report from all credit reporting bureaus whether or not you have received your annual report. These reports are difficult to read at best, and if someone has been racking up a lot of accounts, they may look a lot worse than they actually are. With the report comes a brochure that tells you how to read it. Review it carefully and if you have questions, call for an explanation. Also ask for contact information for any accounts that you do not recognize and contact those companies immediately. Ask the bureaus to remove any fraudulent inquiries and to notify anyone who has received your credit report in the last six months of any disputed or erroneous information.

2. Contact the Social Security Fraud Line: 1–800–772–1213

3. Report the theft to your local police. Get (or make) several copies of their report for use at credit bureaus and financial institutions. Be

sure the police report has a case file number on it.

Dealing with identity theft is a long and time-consuming process. Now would be a good time to start a separate *Life File* folder for your summary notes of conversations with credit bureaus, police, and companies. On each summary sheet, note the dates, names, and phone numbers of all the people you spoke with and the contents of your conversations.

Write letters to all of the credit reporting bureaus, the Social Security Office, and police to confirm your report.

4. Contact all your credit card companies to advise them of fraudulent use and follow up with a letter. (That list in your *Life File* with the toll-free reporting numbers will come in handy.)

This might also be a good time to close some accounts. If you do, make sure the credit card company notes on you file "withdrawn (or closed) at customer request"; otherwise the credit rating bureaus will assume that the card issuer cancelled the card, which will lower your credit rating. When you get your next credit report, make sure it is noted correctly. If you are not due to receive a free annual report for some time, call each bureau and ask them to send you a confirmation.

5. Watch your mail like a hawk. Immediately contact any companies that you did not open accounts with and follow up with a letter.

6. Do not pay any part of a bill that you do not recognize. The case could be made later that if you pay part of it, you are responsible for all of it.

7. Do not file bankruptcy if you can avoid it (see Bankruptcy above). Seek professional help; bankruptcy is a life-altering transaction.

You may want to consult an attorney to determine what legal action you can take against uncooperative creditors and/or credit bureaus. Call your local Bar Association or Legal Aid office to find a specialist in consumer law.

There are other documents beside credit cards that identity thieves are happy to get their hands on: passports (report a loss to the local office of the U.S. State Department; use the photocopy in your *Life File*), telephone calling cards (report to issuing carrier or, if supplied by an employer, advise them), your Social Security card (report a loss at your local Social Security office), and driver's license. Be careful with these things; whether you've memorized your Social Security number or not, do not carry the card around. Professional organization membership cards are also a gateway to identity theft; leave them home and don't forget these organizations on your list of names to call if your purse or wallet is lost or stolen.

Some precautions. Stolen wallets and checkbooks remain the most frequent source of identity theft. When ordering checks, have only your initial(s) and last name printed on them. A thief won't know how you sign your name but the bank will. Use your office address (or a post office box) and office phone number, not your home address or home phone number (or, better yet, none at all); and never, ever have your Social Security number printed on checks.

Never sign your name to the back of a credit card. Instead, in bold block letters write: *Photo ID* or *ID Required.*

When getting a new license or renewing an old one, in most states you are offered the option of using your Social Security number or a random number assigned by computer as the license number. The correct answer to the question is: random number.

When paying bills, never write your complete account number on the memo line, just the last four digits.

When traveling, leave your passport in the hotel

safe; carry a copy with you (only Immigration needs your original passport).

MORTGAGE INFORMATION

When you purchase a residence, lenders generate a boatload of paper mostly on 8.5" x 14" sheets known as legal size. Keep all documents in your *Life File*.

Keep at least the last 12 months' of mortgage statements in your *Life File* and shred any others.

UTILITY STATEMENTS

Keep at least the last 12 statements for all utilities, cable, and telephone in your *Life File* and shred before discarding old statements.

LOANS AND NOTES

Banks and financial institutions aren't the only ones that can make loans. If you lend money to a family member, neighbor, friend, or business associate, it should be agreed to with more than a handshake; they should sign a loan agreement or promissory note. Private loans may or may not involve interest, but they are just as legal as any other loan. Any interest charged may not be higher than that allowed by your state. Keep a copy in your *Life File* and give the original to your attorney (it will become a part of your estate should anything happen and the loan has not been repaid).

PROMISSORY NOTES

When not issued by a bank or other lending institution, a private loan is called a **Promissory Note**. (When a bank issues a promissory note it's called a Certificate of Deposit.) It is a simple form signed and dated by lender and borrower that specifies the amount borrowed, interest rate (if any), how and when repayment will be made, and whether or not the loan is secured with another asset (collateral). Documenting a loan can avoid misunderstandings later about whether the money is a loan or gift and is an important part of your income taxes. The Internal Revenue Service regulates the amount of money one person can give to another as a gift ($10,000) before taxes are imposed. It is important, therefore, to distinguish between a gift and a loan. See the sample *Promissory Note* in the *Appendix.* A copy should be kept in your *Life File* and the original with your attorney in case anything happens and this unpaid debt becomes a part of your estate.

PAY STUBS AND EMPLOYMENT CONTRACTS

Keep your pay stubs for the last year in your *Life File*, especially if you've changed jobs or have multiple employers. Always shred before discarding.

All employees receive contracts that outline the terms of their employment. Employment contracts may be a simple one-page letter that contains information about your job description, work hours, wages, vacation, insurance, sick days or leave, and pensions. It is important to keep it in your *Life File*.

DEEDS, TITLES, LEASES, AND RENTAL AGREEMENTS

These are property issues and should be included in the *Legal* folder of your *Life File*. Deeds and titles are for property you own; lease agreements are for property you own and lease. Rental agreements are for property you rent but do not own.

If you don't use these items, you're home free; if you do, you've already been through the learning process. For newbies, get professional advice before you jump into the deep end of this pool.

FINANCIAL PLANNING
(IT'S YOUR LIFE—*CONTROL IT*)

So far you have organized your paperwork, learned about your financial strengths and weaknesses, sorted out your credit report, and tidied up other old issues. In short, you have made enormous strides in taking control of your life and your future. You are *so* far ahead of the pack, take time to congratulate yourself. Before plunging into the planning process, gift yourself; you've earned it and you deserve it. Treat yourself to a latte, chocolates, a manicure, take a walk in the park (there really is beauty in a tree), or take in a museum (most have free hours). Whatever you do, make it *yours*.

Financial planning is not saving money. Saving money has a lot to do with it, but putting dollars in a savings account is not the whole picture. You can save every spare nickel all year long, but a trip to the hospital can wipe you out over night. Savings accounts, Social Security, pensions, 401(k)s, mutual funds, health savings accounts, and using money wisely now will all add to your financial strength and secure your future.

No matter how small or large your estate, preparing for the future is necessary, not optional. Do you know when a stroke will incapacitate you? When a fire will level your home or a flood wash it away? There are any number of events, a good deal less dramatic than strokes, fires, or floods, that have a profound impact on our lives; and while we cannot anticipate everything, we can take positive steps to assure that unforeseen circumstances don't overwhelm us. Remember the cost/value discussion at *Credit Cards* above? What is the cost and what is the value of planning and preparation? The cost may be trimming down financially now and not being crushed by an unexpected event later; the value is your peace of mind, security, and future.

Among other things, financial planning means choosing investments that are appropriate for your age, tolerance for risk (see below), and expected need for cash. Stocks, for example, often produce greater returns far in the future. You should consider including them in your investment portfolio, especially if you are a number of years away from retirement. "Portfolio" is a general term that refers to the investments (stocks, bonds, CDs) you own. If you are nearing retirement, you may want to invest more conservatively and consider shifting some of your investments from stocks to low-risk investments such as bonds or stable value funds. If you have annuities, stocks, bonds, or mutual funds, you should review them with a professional every year.

Let's look at income and savings plans before turning to investments.

INCOME

What is **Social Security**?

Established in 1935, the Social Security fund has a controversial history. Although over the years it has been expanded to include many more Americans, it was originally funded to offer supplemental retirement income in an age when employers did not offer pensions. Perhaps the circle is closing, as nearly three quarters of a century later, fewer and fewer companies are offering pensions and health benefits to retirees.

Today, Social Security is an essential foundation for retirement that provides partial income, insurance, and survivor's benefits. Although it provides a safety net for most people, Social Security alone is not enough to live on. For an average worker, Social Security benefits will replace only about 40% of their income.

Social Security benefits are earned when you pay into the system at your place of employment. The benefits you will receive at retirement, including Medicare, are calculated based on an estimated 40-year work life. The highest pay received during 35 of those 40 earning years is averaged and the five lowest-earning years are removed from the calculation. The result is the amount of your benefit. Of course, that's an oversimplification that does not include other items (such as taxes) that are factored into the calculation, but is essentially how it works. There is a simple calculator at the Social Security website (www.ssa.gov) that will generate a rough estimate of your expected benefits. If your retirement date is more than five years away, however, you'll need a crystal ball to know what politicians will do to the Social Security fund before your retirement date.

You should be receiving an annual statement from the Social Security Administration that outlines your contributions to date and expected benefits. If you haven't received yours, go to their website to request one.

A spouse may collect Social Security benefits based either on their own work history or as the spouse of an earner (or ex-spouse, provided they were married to the ex-spouse for ten years). Social Security benefits are not automatic; you must apply for them at your local Social Security office. See *Chapter 6, Retirement,* for a fuller discussion.

PERSONAL SAVINGS

Your personal savings are an increasingly important part of your financial strength and it is essential to begin saving early and to invest wisely. A recent survey revealed that half of all U.S. businesses are considering not offering pension plans in the future as well as reducing health care benefits for current employees and retirees. From a different perspective,

America is probably the richest country in the world, but among developed countries we are notoriously poor savers. That has to change. If you don't have some form of savings account today, you need to start one. (See *Chapter 6, Retirement* for information on other types of savings and investment vehicles. A. G. Edwards generates a national and individual Nest Egg Score at www.agedwards.com; click *Home* and *Investor Education*. Take their fourteen-question survey to generate your Nest Egg Score.)

PENSION/RETIREMENT PLANS

What exactly is a **pension plan**? At its simplest level, it is an employer benefit that provides income to employees after retirement. It is "deferred" (will be paid at some future date) compensation. Think of a pension as a series of delayed paychecks that you will receive upon retirement.

Pension plans are generally either defined benefit plans or defined contribution plans. The defined contribution plan is the most common although some plans combine the characteristics of both types.

With a traditional defined benefit pension plan, the benefit an employee will receive upon retirement generally relies on years of service, age at retirement, an employee's average salary over the last three or five years of service, and other factors. For example, if a plan benefit is $100 per month for every year of service; with 30 years of service, the retiree would receive $3,000 per month during their post-retirement lifetime.

Defined contribution plans are usually individual retirement accounts and benefits are based on the amount contributed to the account. Contributions to the pension fund are invested by the fund manager and the returns on these investments (profits or losses) are credited to individual employee accounts. Contributions may be made by the employer, the employee, or both and are subject to Internal Revenue Service limits on how much can be contributed each year. At retirement, the money in the employee's account funds their retirement. Examples of defined contribution plans are Individual Retirement Accounts and 401(k)s.

Pensions and other retirement plans provide a crucial source of income. Unfortunately, today, workers are less likely to earn pensions because they are less likely to work for the same employer long enough to qualify and fewer employers are offering them. Ask your employer's Benefits Officer to review the plan with you. If your pension will not be enough to fund your retirement years, consider starting a savings or investment account to supplement the pension.

The amount of money you will need at retirement varies depending on your lifestyle and expected rate of withdrawal; that is, how much you will need to withdraw from your retirement savings during each year of retirement. Statistically, retirement represents 30% of the average worker's life, or roughly 15 years. Some professionals suggest that you will need 70%-80% of your current annual income for each year of retirement; that is, if your income is $50,000, you will need $35,000 to $40,000 per year during each year of retirement. Based on this assumption, for fifteen years of retirement, a total of $525,000 [$35,000 x 15] or $600,000 [$40,000 x 15] will be required at the time you retire. These numbers aren't as difficult to achieve as you may imagine because much of this money will probably be in interest-baring accounts and interest or dividends will accumulate while you're saving before you retire. Ask your employer's Benefits Officer or your bank or credit union for assistance with planning your expected retirement needs.

Do not assume that Social Security, Medicare, Medicaid, and employer retiree medical benefits will cover all your medical needs. Thirty-six percent of large companies are reducing retiree medical benefits and this trend is likely to trickle down to smaller employers; Social Security and Medicare impose strict income limits (see www.ssa.gov or *Chapter 6, Retirement* for a table of average benefits); and Medicaid is only available to the impoverished. Be sure to consider health care expenses, especially for chronic disease management, when considering your expected retirement needs and review *Chapter 4, Insurance.*

Let's turn now to some of the common types of savings plans. Each has terms and conditions that you should be quite clear about before investing. Always consult a professional. What follows is basic information; there are many, many variations of these plans.

401(k). A **401(k)** is a retirement savings plan to which you may provide all or a portion of the funds and make investment decisions. "Making investment decisions" generally means that when you establish the account, you specify the types of investments you wish to make (for example, the mix of stocks and bonds that are appropriate to your age, expected retirement date, and expected needs at retirement). You may choose to invest all your money in stocks, diversify your portfolio (stocks and bonds), and/or choose bonds. Sometimes employers match all or a part of your contribution. The advantage of a 401(k) is that as well as lowering your taxable income, it is "portable" from one employer to another; a feature not available with traditional pension plans. The disadvantage is that your retirement income will depend on the amount of money in the fund and your personal investing skills.

Individual Retirement Accounts (IRAs). If your employer, or your spouse's employer, does not offer a pension plan or 401(k), it is important that you start making contributions to an **Individual Retirement Account** elsewhere. You can establish an IRA at most banks, brokerage houses, or credit unions. There are several types of IRAs and most require that you be aged 59½ to begin withdrawing money. Withdrawing funds before 59½ ("early" withdrawal) will result in a penalty fee (usually 10% of the total in the IRA). You must begin withdrawing funds at age 70½.

Spousal IRA. A **Spousal IRA** allows full-time homemakers to contribute up to $3,000 per year to an IRA (or $3,500 if they are 50 years old or older).

Nondeductible IRA. A **Nondeductible IRA** is for people who do not qualify for other types of IRAs or who may only be allowed to make partial contributions to an IRA. You may not qualify for an IRA, or may only be allowed to make partial contributions, if you participate in an employer-sponsored or other qualified retirement plan or you don't meet the IRA's income restrictions. Annual contributions to nondeductible IRAs are tax-deferred until retirement. Here, "tax deferred" means that you do not pay income tax on the funds you invest in an IRA (you can deduct them on your annual income tax return); you pay the income tax when you begin to withdraw the funds. Your money compounds free of taxes as long as it remains in the account. Once you withdraw money from the account, it is taxed at ordinary income rates. You may begin to withdraw funds at age 59½ and must begin withdrawing at age 70½.

Roth IRA. A **Roth IRA** provides tax benefits at retirement rather than up front. Contributions cannot be deducted on your annual income tax return, but when you begin withdrawing funds you will not be taxed. Like most IRAs, you may begin to withdraw funds at age 59½ and must begin at age 70½. Roth IRAs are available to everyone whether or not they contribute to a company retirement plan if they meet the income restrictions.

Simplified Employee Pension. A **Simplified Employee Pension** (SEP-IRA) is an Individual Retirement Account for self-employed individuals as well as small business owners and their employees. The owner or worker can contribute up to either 25% of their income or $40,000 per year, whichever is the smaller amount.

Keogh Plan. A **Keogh plan** is a retirement plan for the self-employed that permits them to set aside substantially more than they could with an IRA.

Insurance benefits should also be a part of your financial planning. If you are eligible for Social Security, you will qualify for Medicare that provides coverage for your basic health care needs at retirement. Many people also purchase supplemental insurance to help with costs not covered by Medicare. Contact an insurance agent for information regarding your insurance needs, disability insurance, long-term care insurance, life insurance, and the role they play in your financial and retirement planning. See also *Chapter 4, Insurance.*

INVESTMENTS

Most of us invest in our homes, cars, insurance, and in pensions and mutual funds through our employers. But there are other investment tools that may be of interest. There are many, many variations of the investing instruments defined below; an excellent source of information is Investopedia (www. investopedia.com) where you can find definitions and tutorials on hundreds of investing items. Do as much research as you possibly can before committing to any investment. The research is not easy and only begins when you have identified the kind of investment you want to make.

Annuities, bonds, certificates of deposit, mutual funds, and stocks are all investment vehicles. Contact a professional at a bank, employer, or brokerage firm (or insurance agent in the case of annuities) to discuss the risks involved and what is best for you. For investing purposes, "risk" generally means how much you can afford to lose. "Risk tolerance" means that if you decide to invest $100 that you should be using to pay the rent, you cannot tolerate risking that money because it is not extra (or "discretionary"), it's money you need to live on.

Annuities, bonds, and certificates of deposit

(CDs) all generally work in the same way. They are essentially loans (discussed below) that you make to insurance companies (annuities), corporations, and U.S. government or state municipalities (bonds) or banks, brokerage houses, or deposit brokers (certificates of deposit). They all have four things in common:

1. you lend a fixed amount of money (from $1,000 to millions of dollars);

2. for a fixed length of time, sometimes referred to as its "lifetime" or "term" (from weeks to years);

3. they pay you interest during their lifetime or term; and

4. the full amount of your original investment is returned on its redemption (or "maturity") date.

For example, when you buy a car, after you repay the loan with interest, you get the title to the car. With annuities, bonds, and CDs, the only asset involved is money. While the money is on loan to the bank, government, or insurance company, you receive interest from them; at the end of the loan the original amount of money you loaned is returned. The appeal of these investments is their tax implications; each is taxed differently and to encourage people to invest in them, tax rates are generally favorable.

Of course, whenever you're investing, there is no substitute for research and talking with professionals, but as we shall see, on the whole, there's nothing very mysterious about these investment tools.

ANNUITIES

An **annuity** is offered by an insurance company. They are purchased for a fixed dollar amount for a fixed amount of time at a fixed interest rate. Say, for example, you buy a $10,000 annuity (a fixed dollar amount) that has a 10-year term (a fixed amount of time) at 5% interest (a fixed rate of interest). During the life of the annuity (10 years), interest (5%) is paid to you. When it is cashed in ("redeemed") at maturity (the end of 10 years), your original investment ($10,000) is returned to you. During the life of this type of loan to an insurance company, the interest you receive may be fixed (equal amounts) or variable (varying amounts depending on current interest rates). Interest may be paid monthly, quarterly, semi-annually, annually, or at redemption. Redeeming an annuity before its maturity date (or "early redemption") will result in a penalty, usually between 10% and 20% of the original amount of the annuity. Earnings (interest you receive) are tax deferred during the accumulation phase (in our example, years 1–10); that is, you do not pay taxes on the interest you receive during the life of the annuity. In this example, you will owe taxes on the interest earned at the end of ten years but in the meantime it is not taxed as income.

Annuities should be kept with your attorney or in a safe deposit box. (See *Chapter 6, Retirement,* for information on various types of annuities.) Keep a photocopy in your **Life File**.

BONDS

Bonds are IOUs issued by corporations, the government, or state municipalities (known as "munies") with various risks and rewards. Bonds may be purchased in denominations of $1,000 to $1 million and each bond has a lifetime (from 90 days to many years). When you purchase a bond, you are lending money to the government, corporation, or state that they will pay back in full at the end of the bond's life and in the meantime will pay you interest for the use of your money. **Municipal bonds** are issued by state and local municipalities to fund projects such as new roads and sports arenas and are slightly more risky than U.S. Treasuries (see below) but their tax implications are much broader (consult a professional). Investing in bonds is less risky than investing in stocks.

Government bonds are usually referred to as

"Treasuries" and include Treasury Bills or "T-bills" that mature in 90 days to one year; Treasury Notes (T-Notes) that mature in one to ten years; and Treasury Bonds (T-bonds) that mature in ten or more years. Treasuries are regarded as the safest bond investment because they are backed by the "full faith and credit" of the U.S. Government and interest earned is exempt from state and federal tax so they are often referred to as "tax-free bonds."

All treasuries are sold in denominations of from $1,000 to $1 million and the main difference to investors between T-bills, T-notes and T-bonds are their lifespans. Generally, what your money is used for when you purchase one doesn't matter because it is backed by the U.S. Government and most investors are only interested in turnaround and returns. You may purchase them from the government, a bank, or broker.

Keep your Treasuries with your attorney or in a safe deposit box (and a photocopy in your *Life File*).

CERTIFICATES OF DEPOSIT

Certificates of Deposit (CDs) are purchased from financial institutions. When a bank issues a promissory note it is called a certificate of deposit. Banking institutions, brokerage firms, and independent facilities (known as deposit brokers) offer CDs. CDs are purchased for a fixed amount

SUSAN M. BIGLIONE & MARTHA E. LAISNE

of money, for a fixed amount of time (one month to years) at a fixed interest rate. During the life, or term, of the CD, interest is paid to the owner. Interest payments may be fixed (equal amounts) or variable (depending on the current interest rate). When it is cashed in (redeemed) at maturity, the owner receives their original investment (the amount they paid for the CD). Redeeming a CD before its maturity date (or "early redemption") will result in a penalty fee. The attraction of CDs is that they have higher interest rates than regular bank savings accounts. They can be issued in many denominations. Keep CDs with your attorney or in a safe deposit box (and a photocopy in your *Life File*).

STOCK CERTIFICATES

A rule of thumb when purchasing **stock**: only invest as much money as you can afford to lose. The definition of risk tolerance is worth repeating: "risk tolerance" means that if you decide to invest $100 that you should be using to pay the rent, you cannot tolerate risking that money because it is not extra (or "discretionary"), it's money you need to live on and cannot afford to lose.

With your stock purchase you do not get any guarantees. None. No reputable stockbroker will ever tell you that you are guaranteed a profit. Ever. Period. No debate.

A stock certificate represents a share in a company's ownership. If the company makes a profit, the price of the share will increase. If the company loses money, the price of the share will decrease. If you purchase a stock from a broker or a company (some companies allow you to purchase their shares directly; check with the company Investment Officer) you are entitled to receive a stock certificate for the number of shares you purchase. Stockbrokers, however, keep certificates on file because they assume (read: *hope*) that your purchase is not a one-time trade and send you a statement of account that reflects all purchases, sales, and taxes, not the actual certificates.

"Penny stocks" typically sell for less than $1 or $5 per share (although shares selling for less than $10 may also be referred to as penny stocks). They are issued by companies with a short or erratic history of revenues and earnings and are traded on the Over-the-Counter market as opposed to being traded on the major U.S. exchanges, the New York Stock Exchange, and the American Stock Exchange. They are among the riskiest stocks and are often heavily promoted. These stocks have very poor (if any) liquidity.

"Liquidity" means that something (an asset such as a share of stock, a house, a car, or boat) can easily and readily be converted to cash. When an asset is said to have "good" or "high" liquidity, it means that, if offered for sale, the asset would probably be bought quickly and, therefore, easily converted to cash. Poor liquidity means just the opposite; an asset would be expected to be on the market for a long time before it is sold and converted to cash.

MUTUAL FUNDS

Since **mutual funds** are by far the most common way to invest (an estimated 80 million U.S. investors), let's take a closer look at them.

Mutual funds may be purchased from a mutual fund institution, stockbroker, employer, and are offered as part of pension funds or 401(k)s. The money you contribute to the fund when you purchase a mutual fund share is pooled with other investors' money (mutually owned) and invested by a fund manager. All fund shareholders share in the fund's earnings or losses. There are thousands of funds and all have some level of risk.

When purchased through an employer or as part of a pension plan, there may be restrictions on how much you can contribute each year. If you are 50 years old or older, there is a **catch up provision** that allows you to contribute slightly more each year. You may begin withdrawing funds at age 59½ and must begin withdrawing at age 70½. If your employer offers matching contributions, always contribute enough to get them. Check with your employer's Benefits Manager.

Mutual fund income is earned from dividends (on stocks) and interest (on bonds). A fund may consist of stocks, bonds, or a combination of both. "Asset allocation" is the technical term for the mixture of stocks and bonds in a fund. The fund you choose should be appropriate to achieving your financial goals. (See the descriptions of various types of funds below.) The fund distributes nearly all income earned during a year to its shareholders; some is retained for administrative expenses such as overhead and operating expenses. Any income you receive depends on the number of fund shares you own and how well the fund performs. During the year, if a fund sells stocks or bonds that have increased in value, it generates a "capital gain" that is passed on to shareholders. If capital gains are not clearly explained on your statement, contact the issuer or your Benefits Manager and be sure you understand it because capital gains have important income tax implications.

If the fund performs well, the value of its shares increases. When or if you sell, you can receive either a check for the full amount (less taxes and a proportionate amount of fund expenses), reinvest in more shares, or buy shares in a different fund. Always check the tax implications of a transaction before you make any change; the broker or your employer's Benefit Manager can help.

The important advantage of mutual funds is

SUSAN M. BIGLIONE & MARTHA E. LAISNE

professional management. Most investors don't have the time or experience to manage a portfolio of stocks and bonds. This has nothing to do with an individual's ability to manage money or a portfolio, but rather with how volatile the market is and the incredible amount of research that goes into buying a stock or bond for a fund. Mutual fund firms and banks have entire departments devoted to nothing but investigating and monitoring the stocks and bonds that make up their funds. A mutual fund is an inexpensive way for small investors to have full-time professional managers make and monitor their investments.

Mutual funds are diversified; that is, each fund typically owns many different stocks and/or bonds. The idea is that if a few stocks in the portfolio don't perform well, other stocks and bonds in the fund will do well enough to minimize, or offset, any loss. This is often referred to as "spreading the risk." Funds are also structured to achieve certain goals. There are funds designed for aggressive or medium or conservative growth. To accomplish these goals, the mix of stocks and bonds varies. For example, an aggressive fund may have more stocks than bonds and a conservative fund may have more bonds than stocks. This is known as the fund's asset allocation.

Buying mutual funds is easy and inexpensive. Most banks and employer-sponsored funds can be purchased for $100 a month. Because financial institutions buy and sell large numbers of stocks or bonds for a fund at one time, the costs of these transactions are less than if you did them yourself. A technical term for this process is "economies of scale" which essentially means the more you buy, the less expensive it is. At financial institutions the cost of a buy/sell transaction is a separate expense. Although the cost of trading a hundred shares may be the same as for ten thousand shares, because mutual fund managers trade many thousands of stocks and bonds daily, overall the costs of these transactions are lower. Also, in mutual fund accounts, transaction fees are shared among all fund shareowners.

You can convert fund shares to cash at any time (liquidity) and should clearly understand the income tax implications of any changes. Liquidity means that an asset (your fund share) can be readily converted to cash; unlike, say, a car or home that may or may not sell overnight, a mutual fund share can be converted to cash immediately.

Not all mutual funds are created equal and investing in mutual funds, or anything else that involves putting your hard-earned dollars at risk, must be carefully considered. Get professional advice. There are, of course, disadvantages: some managers are better at their jobs than others; some fund costs are not obvious or clear; and some funds perform better than others because of their basic holdings. There are more than 10,000 funds to choose from and each has its own risks and rewards. On the whole, the higher the expected profits, the higher the risk of losing money. All funds have an investment objective that defines what assets can be held in the fund, what areas of business or government they can invest in, and how they can invest; whether they can invest in high-risk (aggressive) or low-risk stocks and bonds (conservative) or something in between.

Costs are the biggest problem with mutual funds. They eat into your return and the industry is adept at hiding them. Annual fees cover such operating expenses as overhead, salaries, and administration. Transaction and annual fees (also called "loads") are used to compensate brokers or salespeople (commissions), or just to maintain the account. The general industry opinion is: don't buy funds with loads.

Overall, there are three kinds of funds: equity funds invest in stocks; fixed-income funds invest in bonds; and money market funds invest in low-risk short-term debt.

Equity fund. The objective of an **equity fund** is long-term capital growth with some income (for you). There are many types of equity funds because there are many types of stocks. Also known as growth funds, these funds often invest in fast-growing companies and some equity funds are considered high risk. Equity funds that invest only in companies in the same industry are called specialty funds (see below).

Fixed income fund. A **fixed income fund**. provides fixed periodic payments and eventually returns the principal. An example would be a fund composed of fixed-rate government bonds. (With a fixed-rate government bond that you purchase for, say, $1,000 at 5% for one year, you would earn $50 when the bond matures and also receive your $1,000 back.) Fixed income funds offer low returns because they guarantee income.

Money market fund. **Money market funds** consist mainly of short-term debt, such as Treasury bills. Returns are generally low, about twice what you would earn on a regular bank checking/savings account and a little less than on a certificate of deposit, but their attraction is fast turnaround. These funds are considered low risk.

OTHER MUTUAL FUNDS

Asset allocation fund. Similar to a balanced mutual fund (see next) but the manager of an **asset allocation fund** decides on the percentage of the mix of stocks and bonds in the fund. That is, when a fund is created, the terms and objectives of the fund are clearly defined and identify what kinds of stocks and bonds, and what percentage of each, may be included in the fund. The fund manager must comply with these restrictions when purchasing or selling stocks and bonds. An asset allocation fund is different in that the fund manager is solely responsible for the mix of stocks and bonds.

Balanced fund. A variety of the asset allocation class of mutual funds, these funds attempt to provide a "balanced" mixture of safety and income by investing in a combination of fixed-income (bonds) and equities (stocks). A typical **balanced fund** contains 60% stocks and 40% bonds while more aggressive growth funds would have different percentage mixes, say, 80% stocks and 20% bonds, and a conservative fund would have 80% bonds and 20% stocks (also see *Lifestyle funds* below).

To assure that the fund you invest in achieves your financial and investment goals, always carefully discuss with a professional the mix of stocks and bonds in the fund; the income you receive from the fund depends on the percentage of stocks and bonds in it.

Bond fund. There are many types of bonds to invest in: at one end of the scale, junk bonds are very high-risk **corporate bonds**, while at the other end, government bonds are low-risk. **Bond funds** may pay higher returns than certificates of deposit and money market funds but are also subject to interest rate risk; if interest rates go up, the value of the fund goes down.

Global and *International funds.* **Global funds**

invest anywhere in the world while an **international fund** only invests outside of its home country. Both of these types of funds have advantages and disadvantages depending on their home country or the country in which they invest. Within these types of funds, regional funds focus on specific areas of the world or specific countries.

Income fund. **Income funds** are designed to provide income on a steady basis. These funds invest primarily in government and corporate bonds. Because the objective of these funds is to provide a steady cash flow, they appeal to conservative investors and retirees or those approaching retirement.

Index fund. **Index funds** consist of stocks and bonds that match, or track, the components of a market index such as the Standard & Poor's 500 or the Russell 2000.

Socially-responsible fund. **Socially-responsible funds** (or ethical funds) only invest in companies that meet certain guidelines and usually do not invest in industries such as tobacco, alcohol, weapons, or nuclear power.

Specialty fund. **Specialty funds** concentrate their investments in a certain sector of the economy such as finance or technology or health care and are also referred to as sector funds.

The latest trend in mutual funds is **Lifestyle funds** These funds feature an asset mix appropriate to individual investors. The object of the fund may be conservative, moderate, or aggressive growth depending on an investor's age, income, the level of risk the investor wants to take with their money, the purpose of the investment, and the length of time until the principal will be withdrawn. Aggressive growth is appropriate for investors in their twenties, and conservative growth is appropriate for older investors. A shareholder's participation in these funds is reviewed annually, and the mix of stocks and bonds is adjusted as people age, shifting from aggressive to moderate to conservative growth.

ROLLING OVER

When you leave one employer and move to another, you may "**roll over**" your mutual fund, IRA, or 401(k). To minimize any loss or incur tax penalties in the process, you need professional advice. The Benefits Officer of your current (or future) employer will help you make this important financial transition. Twentysomethings almost always forget to do this or are intimidated by the paperwork. Don't be. This is quite possibly one of the simplest financial transactions. Whether you're 20 years old or 50, don't leave any of your money on the table for someone else to pick up; you're just moving it from one place to another and you want to be sure that you're not subject to income tax or penalties. You have sixty days to get it done; plenty of time to get advice.

SAVING ON THE MORTGAGE

Mortgage refinancing may be something you're considering. Basically, refinancing depends on how much you will save each year and for how many years you will save; and makes sense if you expect to own your home for many years. It does not make sense, of course, to spend $5,000 in closing costs to save $1,000 a year if you will be moving in a year or two. Shop for a good deal and understand all the costs before you make a commitment. Some refinancers have a standard mortgage initiation fee and others do not charge closing costs. Be very clear on these fees; some mortgagers will keep the initiation fee whether or not you complete a refinance.

When contemplating refinancing, consider if you need a **fixed rate** or **adjustable-rate mortgage** (referred to as an "ARM"; see also *Chapter 6, Retirement*). A fixed-rate mortgage suits most people. It is the least tricky to shop for and adds an element of certainty to financial planning. With a fixed-rate loan, the interest rate remains the same throughout the life of the loan; whether or not interest rates rise or fall has no impact on the loan or your monthly payment. If rates fall significantly (what are the chances?), you can refinance at a lower rate. Interest rates on an adjustable-rate mortgage move up or down with the current interest rate and any change in interest rates affects your monthly mortgage payment.

Some mortgage holders offer the option to pay down a 30-year loan in fifteen years by making bi-monthly payments. Investigate this option carefully to make sure it makes sense for you, if you can afford it, and what are the exact terms (are you locked in to two full payments a month?). If the terms of your current loan agreement allow it, you may also be able to make payments on the principal (only) at your convenience without a prepayment penalty. You may send the lender a check for any amount that is convenient *for you* and mark the check "Principal Only." The amount will be applied only to the principal and will reduce the total amount of dollars in interest you eventually pay, but it does not reduce the interest rate. If you do not mark the check "Principal Only," it will simply be applied as your next mortgage payment or part of it, meaning that most of it will be applied to interest.

The interest rate on a 30-year mortgage is usually higher than for other mortgages. A conservative choice may be to shoulder a slightly higher monthly payment for a 15-year loan. The advantage is paying much less interest over the life of the loan and owning your home in half the time. This would be appropriate if you intend to sell the property in less than fifteen years; why pay more interest on a 30-year loan if you will be gone in five years.

Paying down your current mortgage is an unexciting way to invest, but it is a smart one.

It is also completely safe. Suppose you have a 6% mortgage with twenty years left to go (interest you pay on a mortgage is tax deductible). If you receive a tax refund, a bonus at work, an inheritance, or a legal settlement, apply it to the principal (only). It is never rational, though, to borrow at 24% interest from a bank or on a credit card to pay any part of the balance of a 6% loan.

Using the equity in your home to pay debts or fund retirement is becoming easier. There are limits on who can obtain a home equity loan and it is important to use the money wisely. What a coincidence! The title of the next section is *Use Your Home Equity Wisely*.

USE YOUR HOME EQUITY WISELY

One of legendary actress Bette Davis' famous lines was: "Fasten your seatbelts; it's going to be a bumpy ride." *When Life Changes Forever* is the road leveler. If a home equity loan was too complicated for the average person, no one would do it.

The *Introduction* states: "If you have been running a household and/or a small business, there isn't much more we, or anyone else, can tell you about money and how to use it." It's true and the aim here is not to reinvent the wheel but if this is new territory for you, keep going, it's a simple concept.

Let's get the definitions out of the way first. From

the title, "your home" is what you're putting on the line and "equity" is the difference between how much your home is worth (its value) and how much you owe on the mortgage (its cost).

When you buy a house, the money you put down is your initial **home equity** With every mortgage payment you make, the amount of the loan decreases and your equity increases. Think of a seesaw: as you add weight (mortgage payments) to the high end, it gradually goes down and the other end (your equity) rises.

To get a home equity loan you need "collateral." **Collateral** is an asset that you give the lender to keep until you've repaid the loan. When the loan is repaid, you get the asset back. If you don't repay the loan, the lender keeps the asset and gets their money back by selling it (called "**foreclosure**").

A home equity loan is a second mortgage in sheep's clothing. The bank or lender is buying whatever equity you have built up in your home. You are selling your home. You receive a one-time lump sum or regular payments that you can spend any way you want and the loan is usually repaid when you sell your home, if not before. Most people use the money for home improvements, debt consolidation, tuition, or medical or other expenses. Of course, there are a lot more details, but essentially that's it.

Another type of equity loan is the **reverse mortgage** It is for homeowners age 62 and older who wish to borrow against the equity they have built up in their homes. It pays the homeowner a line of credit, lump sum, or monthly payments. The homeowner does not need to repay the loan as long as they live in the home; it is repaid when the owner sells the home or when the homeowner dies and the loan is paid off by the homeowner's estate. For more information, visit the American Association of Retired Person's (AARP) website at aarp.org and search *reverse mortgage*)

Using the money wisely is the trick.

Many people run up a lot of credit card debt and use a home equity or reverse mortgage loan to pay off or consolidate these debts. This is not a very good idea. You have paid off credit card debt that you could have paid without risking your home. Now you are risking your home that you will be able to repay the new home equity loan. You haven't gotten out of debt, you've added to it. Using the reverse mortgage loan does not involve monthly repayments but you have exchanged your home for the loan.

Being free of credit card debt is good, but don't be tempted to use the cards again because they have zero balances. Get rid of them; they are what got you into poor financial shape in the first place.

Using a home equity loan to pay medical bills is also not a very good idea. The reason has to do with collateral. Credit cards and medical bills are "unsecured" debts, which means that you have not pledged another asset (a home, for example) to guarantee that you'll repay them. Using your home as collateral to obtain an equity loan to pay off these debts means that if you fail to repay it, you are risking foreclosure or a lien on your home. This is especially tricky for medical bill payments. Even after insurance has been exhausted, there is no guarantee that you will not incur more medical expenses, unlike credit card debt over which you have some control.

Using your home equity money to buy big-ticket items (cars or boats) is definitely a bad idea. Most assets depreciate; that is, over time they lose value. A new car loses more than 10% of its value as it's driven off the dealer's lot. Real estate may be an exception, but there is still no guarantee that it will increase in value; sooner or later that scenic property on the Atlantic low-tide line or the San Andreas Fault will simply disappear.

Flopping your home equity loan check down on stocks or commodities is nutty. If the stock trade goes south, it will take your investment and home with it; you still have to repay the loan, and in case of trading commodities, you could owe considerably more before the trade closes. Good luck with that one.

Making upgrades and repairs to your home increases its value and is an effective use of the money. Of course, there are many valid uses for a home equity loan that may not add much value: tuition, for example. It adds value to the student's future income potential, although as a parent a second mortgage isn't adding much value to your life. The point is to think very carefully about what you will use the money for and how much risk you are willing to take with the asset you use as collateral. Make the money work for you to increase value in some way.

CHAPTER 3: *Medical*

WHO'S WHO AND WHAT'S WHAT

Of all the decisions we make, medical decisions may be the most heartrending and frustrating. Most people have only the merest knowledge of how the body functions and a lot less about the medical/insurance world. A trip to a hospital can be likened to Alice falling into the rabbit hole; the environment is odd, the language makes little sense, and we make decisions based on the advice of total strangers.

There is a lot of help available.

The latest effort to involve consumers in their care is the Hospital Compare website sponsored by the U.S. Department of Health and Human Services (www.hospitalcompare.hhs.gov). Created to provide "information on how well the hospitals in your area care for all their adult patients with certain medial conditions," you can look at the (easy-to-read) statistics to determine how well local hospitals treat some ailments as compared to national averages. Not just statistics, this website defines the illness and its recommended treatment(s) and gives you an idea of how your local hospital stacks up when compared to national averages. This would be very helpful if, for example, you had a choice of hospitals, you would prefer the one that has better average success rates. In addition, this website has links to other informative sites.

Another is Quality Check (www.qualitycheck.org) that identifies a wide range of types of care provided by various facilities across the nation. That is, if you need information on assisted living, cancer, types of disease care, medical supplies, or a long list of other items, this website offers information on where to obtain these services or equipment in your area, as well as their accreditation by the Joint Commission (formerly Joint Commission on Accreditation of Healthcare Organizations). The website is extensive and informative.

If for no other reason to access these sites, it may be important to review the local information provided before you make decisions about what facility or supplier you will use.

Nevertheless, there is a great deal of basic information to add to your medical map, so let's hit the road.

YOUR LIFE FILE

MEDICAL RECORDS

You are your own or a loved one's best advocate. One thing you can do for yourself, or anyone being treated at any medical facility for any reason, is to get as much information as possible, and to keep notes. They don't have to be elaborate but they should include such information as dates of hospitalization or doctors visits, contact information for those participating in the care, a list of medications, and the dates and names of any procedures performed in a doctor's office, hospital, or by a lab. This will assist you in discussing your own, or a loved one's, medical situation and future care.

Medical records contain a detailed list of everything that happens to a patient during their visit to a doctor's office or stay at a hospital or other medical facility. They contain a "diagnosis" of what the doctor thinks the problem is, a detailed description of the steps taken to fix the problem, and a "prognosis," or what the doctor thinks the patient's outcome will be. It is from these records that the billing department gets the data to charge the patient or the insurance company for every tissue, aspirin, medication, lab test, X-ray, massage, or piece of equipment. (Also refer to *Chapter 4, Insurance.*)

You are entitled to see your medical records

whenever you request them from the hospital records department.

LIST OF MEDICATIONS

The simplest way to get a complete list of medications is to request one from your pharmacist; they have it in their computers and pride themselves on helping patients and families. If you are not the patient, you will need to establish your relationship to the patient before pharmacists will release their records. Most pharmacists will analyze medications and alert you to any unsafe interactions. Keep the list or pharmacy printout in your *Life File* and update regularly. Shred obsolete copies.

LIST OF PHYSICIANS

Create a list of all physicians that attend to your family and their contact numbers. Keep it in your *Life File*.

LIST OF MEDICAL FACILITIES

If you or others receive services from multiple health care facilities, list their names, addresses, and telephone numbers. Also include contact information for individuals at each facility; keep it up-to-date and in your *Life File*.

These may seem to be yet more additions to an

endless list of lists, but when seconds count in the "golden hour," how long would it take to piece it together? Although opinions vary, the golden hour refers to the first sixty minutes after a major trauma. If a victim can receive hospital care within one hour of a trauma, their chances of survival are improved. Or, if you are in an emergency situation and can't communicate, this list will be invaluable. Protect yourself and your family.

Who's Who and What's What

When it comes to the "in sickness and in health" part of your marriage vows, men are definitely from a galaxy far, far away and generally recoil from the punishing work of caring for the sick or dying, while women are nurturers. But either or both of you can be called to active duty overnight. A stroke, fall, or heart attack, and before you know it the hospital is discharging an enfeebled loved one to your doorstep.

You have just made a career change: you are going into nursing or physical therapy without a single day of training. The basic information you need to bathe or move a patient from bed to chair or to alleviate pain is beyond your experience and knowledge. Don't panic: help, and lots of it, is available.

DISCHARGE PLANNERS

One of the most important sources of information in the medical community is the **Medical Discharge Planner** This person (or department) is vital to the patient, you, and your family. All hospitals have someone who performs this function, and they have a wealth of knowledge about local care facilities, the levels of care provided, the costs of each, and a lot more. It's their job to be well informed not only about care facilities, but the ins and outs of Medicare, Medicaid, and private insurance. They also know what services are available locally and how to obtain them. Even if a patient is not currently at their hospital, they'll be glad to help you, and getting their advice can save you a lot of time and anxiety. Make friends with them; they're nice people.

The following are some functions Discharge Planners perform. The list is not comprehensive but will give you an idea of what to expect.

Discharge planning begins within 24 hours of admission and the patient and family are kept informed of all discharge plans.

Patient and family receive a discharge instruction sheet that is also given to all individuals and organizations responsible for providing continuing care. These discharge instructions generally include:

* List of medications

* Requisitions for laboratory tests or other studies

* Recommendations about lifestyle choices and changes regarding activities, exercise, and diet

* Self-care instructions (such as wound care, colostomy maintenance, insulin administration)

* When and how to obtain care or treatment after discharge

* Emergency information

* Managing continuing care (scheduling home services, visiting nurses, aides, obtaining walkers, canes, oxygen, and other necessities)

SOCIAL WORKERS

Another patient ally is the **Social Worker** In the medical setting, they help people function in their new (and sometimes threatening) environment, deal with relationships, and help resolve personal and family issues. Social workers routinely see patients suddenly faced with minor and life-threatening situations. They are well aware of the difficulties confronting patients and their families and expert at easing their transition. Social workers usually have offices at large hospitals and/or regularly visit health care facilities.

CAREGIVER SUPPORT

If you become a caregiver there's a lot to learn. Remember, you are the consumer, you want to know the doctor, hospital and health care facility's track records, what all of your options are (in clear, concise language), and to make your own choices. You demand as much when purchasing a TV.

Let's begin to build the medical roadmap with basic definitions. There's a lot of caregiver terminology; most of it is related to finances and what Medicare, Medicaid, and insurance will and won't pay.

Long ago, "levels" of care were determined by a patient's needs and a doctor's recommendation, but over the years the lines have become fuzzy and they are now only loose guidelines. Nevertheless, you should have some understanding of the terms to determine your needs.

First, all care and levels of care are based on a timeframe. Care will be either short- or long-term.

Short-term care refers to 90 days or less and, depending on the situation, may or may not include a range of services.

Long-term care refers to an indefinite time and usually includes a comprehensive range of medical, personal, and social services. You may need long-term care at any age. It may be provided at home, in the community, at assisted living facilities, or at nursing homes. Medicare's partial definition of long-term care is: "…a variety of services that include medical and non-medical care to people with **chronic illnesses** or disabilities." Generally, Medicare does not pay for long-term care.

In most states, Medicaid pays for some long-term care services at home and in the community. Eligibility varies and is based on income, personal resources, and covered services.

LEVELS OF CARE

Levels of care are terms generally used by physicians to outline what care a patient needs and by insurance companies to refer to where treatment is received.

In an insurance policy, levels of care refers to where care is given or received. Those locations are:

Doctor's office, hospital, or clinic
Emergency room
Acute hospital care
Specialty hospital
Rehabilitation facility
Skilled nursing facility (also referred to as a Subacute rehabilitation facility)
Nursing home

In the medical setting, levels of care refer to what services are provided.

The distinctions are based on what procedures an insurer will pay for and who performs them; insurers will not pay for treatments at a facility or those that are performed by people who do not meet their guidelines.

Basic care. **Basic care** indicates services required to maintain the **activities of daily living** personal care assistance (eating, dressing, bathing, toilet), walking (ambulation), as well as supervision and safety (access to 24-hour emergency care), and social and recreational activities. Pretend you have a broken leg encased in an ankle-to-hip cast. Even fit persons would have difficulty moving from one room to another and bathing. These activities are important considerations in the terms of an insurance policy (see *Chapter 4, Insurance*).

Basic care may be provided by a family member, an aide, or a visiting nurse.

> A **Registered Nurse** is a professional nurse who often supervises the tasks of Licensed Practical Nurses, Licensed Vocational Nurses, orderlies, and nursing aides. They provide direct care and make decisions regarding plans of care.
> A **Licensed Practical Nurse** or Licensed Vocational Nurse, has enough training to be licensed by a state to perform routine care.
> A **nurse's aide** assists a nurse in tasks that require little formal training.

These are hardly the only services they perform;

they are extraordinary people with an extraordinary knowledge of all sorts of hospital and care issues and are willing to share that information. Ask them.

Custodial care. **Custodial care** offers services above basic care but less than skilled care. Non-professionals (non-skilled, non-certified workers) provide help with bathing, dressing, eating, getting in or out of a bed or chair, moving around, and using the bathroom. It may also be performed by a family member, an aide, or visiting nurse. Medicare does not pay for custodial care.

Intermediate care. Typically, **intermediate care** is medically necessary and provided by licensed professionals under the direct orders of a physician. This type of care is provided on an occasional basis, that is, if, for example, a patient is moved from a health care facility to their home, a licensed professional may supervise the move, or they may visit the patient once a week for a month. It is not ongoing daily care.

Personal care. **Personal care** is assistance with walking, bathing, dressing, and grooming services, bowel, bladder, and menstrual care, repositioning or transfer, skin care, range of motion exercises, feeding, hydration (liquids), and help with self-administered medications. Personal medical care professionals are hired and paid privately.

Skilled care. This level of care requires the services of, and may only be provided by, a Registered Nurse and/or other specially trained professionals for treatments and procedures on a regular base. **Skilled care** is around-the-clock care for convalescent and long-term care patients and may include intravenous injections, monitoring and upkeep of feeding tubes, oxygen, sterile bandaging, and/or physical, occupational, and respiratory therapies. Medicare pays only for medically eligible necessary care at skilled nursing facilities or at home. If the care is medically necessary, some Medicare Advantage plans (formerly Medicare + Choice) offer limited skilled nursing facility and home-care coverage. For more information on these plans, see the Medicare website www.medicare.gov.

Skilled nursing care. Only Registered Nurses or other medical professionals may provide skilled nursing care. Examples of **skilled nursing care** services include intravenous injections, feeding tubes maintenance, oxygen, and changing sterile dressings. A skilled nursing care facility is staffed by rehabilitation and other related health service professionals. Generally, Medicare does not pay for skilled nursing care.

CARE FACILITIES

There are many types of care facilities to choose from depending on the type of care needed, hospital affiliation, expected length of stay, location, religious affiliation, activities provided, and costs. Prices vary considerably.

At home. Your home or the home of the patient may be termed a health care facility and there are many home service programs available. Many people need the level of care provided by a nursing facility but prefer to remain at home. These patients, particularly stroke victims experiencing memory loss, do better in their home environment and have a shorter convalescence period. A Visiting Nurse or therapist visits the home to provide treatment or instruction for patient and family. Treating patients at home might include assistance with intravenous medications and equipment such as oxygen and walkers.

Medicare offers limited access to two programs for those who need a comprehensive range of medical and social services: **Program of All-Inclusive Care for the Elderly** (PACE) and Social Managed Care Plans.

PACE is an optional Medicare and Medicaid benefit available in some states under Medicaid. There are eligibility and screening requirements and it is primarily offered to older citizens frail enough to meet their state's standards for nursing home care. It features comprehensive medical and social services that can be provided at an adult daycare center, at home, or at an inpatient facility. Check with your local Medicaid office for more information.

Social Managed Care plans are insurance plans offered by HMOs (Health Management Organizations) that participate in Medicare and provide a full range of Medicare benefits. There are four Social Managed Care plans: Kaiser Permanente, Portland, Oregon; SCAN, Long Beach, California; Elderplan, Brooklyn, New York; and Health Plan of Nevada, Las Vegas, Nevada. All plans have eligibility requirements and offer a full range of services and products. Premiums vary from plan to plan. See www.medicare.gov/Nursing/Alternatives/SHMO. asp (accessed 3/25/07) for an overview of each.

There are many home services available locally: Meals on Wheels, visiting and shopper services, transportation, personal care, chore assistance, and a variety of activities at senior centers, usually provided free or at low cost to qualified individuals. Local organizations, called Area Agencies on Aging, coordinate these activities to promote the independence and dignity of older adults. The **Elder Care Locator** can help you find **community services** in your area (www.eldercare.gov or 1–800–677–1116). Depending on your situation, Medicare, private insurance, and Medicaid may pay for some home care costs.

The following community-based services may be available in your area:

* Adult daycare (see below)

* Senior centers (see below)

* Financial management (assistance with bill paying and other routine financial matters)

* Telephone reassurance (periodic calls to assure a patient's welfare)

* Case management (assistance with obtaining health care services)

EMERGENCY MEDICAL RESPONSE SYSTEMS

Emergency medical response systems for in-home use are available from reputable firms. Also referred to as a **Personal Emergency Medical Response Systems** they are electronic devices used to summon help in an emergency.

They consist of a small radio transmitter (carried or worn by the user), a console connected to a landline telephone and an emergency response center that monitors calls. When medical, fire, or police help is needed, the user presses the transmitter button that sends a signal to the console. The console automatically dials the monitoring center or one or more pre-selected numbers and most consoles can dial even if the phone is off the hook.

At the monitoring center, personnel try to determine the nature of the emergency and may review the user's medical history and check to see who should be notified. If the center personnel cannot contact the user or determine if or what emergency exists, it will alert local emergency services to go to the home.

Systems can be purchased, rented, or leased. Most insurance companies and, in most states, Medicare or Medicaid will not pay for the purchase of equipment; the few insurance companies that do, require a doctor's recommendation. Some hospitals and social service agencies may subsidize low-income users. Installation and monthly fees are required.

Rentals are available through national manufacturers, local distributors, hospitals, and social service agencies.

Leases can be long-term or lease-to-purchase. Review the lease terms carefully, especially cancellation clauses, for any fees or other charges. Also review the warranty and any service contract for replacement or repair charges.

Before signing any contract, shop to compare costs and check with the local consumer protection agency or Better Business Bureau. Before deciding on a system:

* Check out several systems; be sure the one you choose is easy to use.

* Make sure it works from every point in and around your home (that is, the signal range includes your front and back yards).

* Can you use the same system if you move to another city or state?

* How and how often is the system tested in the home?

* Is monitoring available 24 hours a day, 7 days a week?

* What is the average response time?

ADULT DAYCARE

Daycare programs offer visits to local adult daycare facilities a few times a week and some provide transportation. Elder Services in your city or town can give you details. Some Medicaid programs pay for this type of care.

Adult daycare centers may be public, private, non-profit, or for-profit. They provide older adults with an opportunity to get out of the house to receive mental and social stimulation and give regular caregivers a much-needed break. They may offer physical, occupational, and speech therapy, and may be staffed by a Registered Nurse and/or other health care professionals. Typically, nutritious meals that accommodate special diets and afternoon snacks are provided.

Two other types of adult daycare are the **social adult daycare** that usually requires a physician's health assessment before admission, and **senior**

daycare for seniors with Alzheimer's or other types of dementia.

NURSING CARE FACILITIES

There is a wide variety of nursing care facilities. Each depends on the level of care required, and your choice may be influenced by location, hospital affiliation, services offered, religious affiliation, anticipated length of stay, and cost. All facilities must be accredited by the Joint Commission on the Accreditation of Healthcare Organizations (JCAHO). (To find accreditation information on nursing homes in your area, visit the JCAHO website, www.jcaho.org.) Nursing homes offer long-term care, short-term intensive rehabilitation, and short-term terminal care. They are permanent residences for people too frail or ill to live at home or for temporary residence during a recovery period.

Selecting the right care facility is a decision based as much on emotion as on finances. It is important for you and family members to visit the facility to make sure it meets your needs before making a decision. By the time you get to the reception desk, you will have formed an impression of whether or not you are comfortable with the facility. Trust your instincts.

All facilities are rated by professional examiners on a long list of items (about 150). The Centers for Medicare and Medicaid Services (CMS) is the component of the Federal Government's Department of Health and Human Services that oversees Medicare (federal) and Medicaid (state) programs. State governments oversee the licensing of nursing homes, and Congress has established minimum requirements for their operation. CMS contracts with each state to conduct annual onsite inspections to determine if its nursing homes meet the minimum Medicare and Medicaid quality and performance standards. All states have their own regulations, but the questions below will give you a feel for what is expected.

* Are visiting hours convenient for family and friends?

* Is it certified by Medicare and Medicaid?

* Is it and its current administrator licensed?

* Do residents appear clean and well groomed?

* Are rooms, halls, dining areas, and grounds well kept and clean?

* Do residents have the same staff on a daily basis, and is there enough staff available to assist all residents?

* Is staff cheerful and pleasant, and are patients able to communicate with staff in their native language?

* Does it have an active resident and/or family council?

* Are there a variety of activities?

* Does it provide the services you need?

* What are the basic costs? What services are included in the basic cost? What additional costs are there?

It is important to review the nursing home's last annual state inspection report. What problems did the examiners find and were they fixed? Your loved one will be there many hours when you are not; you want to be sure that their environment is as safe as possible and that caregivers are as interested in giving patients as much care as you would.

At the bottom tier, facilities use unskilled (and perhaps undocumented) workers and are a lot more interested in collecting a check than in patient welfare. Definitely do your homework.

Given the increasing need for care facilities, the industry is growing rapidly, but not fast enough to keep pace with a fast-growing population of elderly, and it is not uncommon to use a short-term care facility while awaiting accommodations in a long-term care facility.

NURSING HOMES

Nursing homes are residential assistance facilities that provide a variety of levels of care to those unable to care for themselves. Payment is usually monthly, and costs vary widely with the levels of care provided, location, medical staffing, and institutional affiliations (associations with local hospitals).

Some nursing homes provide Medicare-reimbursed skilled care (see above and the *Glossary* for a definition of skilled care) after an injury or hospital stay for a limited time if eligibility requirements are met. For more information, see the Medicare booklet, *Medicare Coverage of Skilled Nursing Facility Care,* at www.medicare.gov. Medicare does not reimburse for most nursing home care or services.

Bed-hold policy Sometimes referred to as a "bed reservation." If a care facility resident is hospitalized, nursing homes will keep the patient's bed vacant until they return, provided they return within a certain number of days. The length of time they will "hold" or "reserve" the bed depends on Medicare, Medicaid, the terms of the patient's insurance policy, the length of the hospital stay, or the patient's ability to pay daily charges privately. Bed-hold policies are regulated in some states.

Medicare only covers a maximum of three days. When a Medicare patient is hospitalized longer than three days, they are entitled to be readmitted to a nursing home—when a new bed becomes available.

If a patient (or their family) wishes to pay the nursing home privately, the patient (or their family) must pay for each day the patient is absent from the residence beyond the three-day Medicare limit. When private insurance pays for nursing home residence while a patient is hospitalized, the number of days they may be absent from the residence is stated in the policy. When the maximum number of days of absence is reached, an insurer will no longer reimburse the nursing home, and the nursing home will reassign the bed to a different patient unless the patient (or their family) pays the daily nursing charges.

Alternates. Some patients require less than skilled care or skilled care for only a brief time. Following is a list of living arrangements at different levels of care that may be available in your community.

Subsidized Senior Housing There are federal and state programs available that reimburse for elder housing for those with low to moderate incomes. Some subsidized senior housing facilities offer assistance with tasks such as shopping and laundry. Residents generally live independently in an apartment or room within the senior housing complex with communal dining. These programs include assisted living and board and care facilities.

Assisted Living Medicare does not pay for

assisted living care. Assisted living arrangements are residential facilities that may have private rooms or apartments and communal dining. Appointments for health care and social services; help with bathing, dressing, toileting, cooking, laundry, or reminders to take medications; and recreational activities may be provided. Not all assisted living facilities provide the same services. Residents pay a regular monthly fee and additional fees for some services. Costs vary widely depending on the size of the living areas, services provided, type of help needed, and location in the community. A 2005 survey of Assisted Living Costs found that the national average monthly rate for an individual residing in an assisted living facility was $2,905, and since then, no reliable data could be found, but at a 5% annual increase, the presumed 2008 monthly cost would be $3,302. In some states, Medicaid programs pay for some services but only for low-income residents who would otherwise qualify for more expensive nursing home care.

Board and Care Facilities   These **group living arrangements** are for people who cannot live independently and do not require nursing services. Since many of these facilities do not receive Medicare or Medicaid reimbursement, they are not strictly monitored. They may offer a wider range of services than independent living options: most provide help with activities of daily living (eating, dressing, walking, bathing, and toileting). In some situations, private long-term care insurance and other types of assistance programs may help to pay for this type of living arrangement. The monthly charge is usually a percentage of a patient's income. For local information, see the National Association of Area Agency on Aging at www.n4a.org for an Eldercare Locator link.

CONTINUING CARE RETIREMENT COMMUNITIES

Continuing care retirement communities provide several levels of care: from independent living apartments to skilled nursing care in an affiliated nursing home. "Zoned" for various levels of care (individual homes or apartments, assisted living facilities, and nursing care sites), residents move from one level of care (or zone) to another (higher level of care) within the community. Many continuing care retirement communities require an entry payment prior to admission to a different zone in addition to monthly fees and often require that residents use the nursing home component. A disadvantage is that once admitted to one level of care, the contract may require that a patient move to the next higher level of care within the community, whether or not it is appropriate for the patient, or pay a penalty. If nursing care is needed, the contract may require that residents first use lower levels of service before being admitted to the nursing care component. For more information, contact the American Association of Homes and Services for the Aging (www.aahsa.org or 202–783–2242).

To check the record of a continuing care retirement community's nursing home component and the community's accreditation status, go to the Commission on Accreditation of Rehabilitation Facilities (www.carf.org), the Administration on Aging (www.aoa.gov), and the American Association of Homes and Services for the Aging (www.aahsa. gov).

RESPITE CARE

For family members or friends who provide at-home care. It allows the caregiver to take a break by providing a substitute caregiver. **Respite care** can be provided in the home or in a nursing home. Respite care is not reimbursed by most insurers but may be covered by Medicare in conjunction with covered hospice care offered by some nursing homes.

HOSPICE CARE

For terminally ill patients nearing the end of life, **hospice care** may include nursing care, pain control, spiritual or emotional counseling, symptom management, and family counseling. A patient may be at home, at a hospital, hospice care facility, or skilled nursing home. A team of doctors, nurses, home health aides, social workers, counselors, and trained volunteers help patients and family cope with illness. The goal is to care for, not cure, a patient. Payment is usually monthly depending upon the level of care and use of premises. Medicare may cover medical and support services such as nursing care, medical and social services, physician services, counseling, homemaker services, and others. Medicare covers at-home hospice care (but not 24-hour assistance). Medicare does not cover room and board for general hospice services at a nursing or hospice facility. For more information or to find a hospice in your area, contact the National Hospice and Palliative Care Organization at 1–800–658–8898 or www.nhpco.org.

MEDICARE

Medicare is the national health insurance program for Social Security recipients who are U.S. citizens, permanent residents, over 65 years of age, or under 65 years old with permanent disabilities or end-stage renal disease.

Since Medicare is not welfare, personal income and assets are not considered when determining eligibility or benefits. Like Social Security, the amount of benefits you are eligible for under Medicare is determined by the number of "quarters" worked. (See *What is Social Security?* in *Chapter 2,*

Finance; Social Security Benefits below; and *Earned Social Security Benefits* in *Chapter 6, Retirement*).

Medicare like private insurance plans, pays a portion of the cost of some medical care and the patient pays a deductible (a fixed amount that must be paid out-of-pocket before benefits will begin) and co-payments that are a portion of a health care provider's cost shared by the patient. (See also *Chapter 4, Insurance.*) For a complete list of benefits, see *Your Medicare Benefits* published by the U.S. Department of Health and Human Services and on their website at www.medicare.gov/Publications/Pubs/pdf/10116.pdf (accessed 3/25/07).

Medicare has two basic coverage plans: Part A (insurance for hospital costs) and Part B (insurance for medical costs). Part A covers inpatient hospital care, hospice care, in-patient care at a skilled nursing facility, and some home health care services. Part B covers medical care and services provided by doctors and other medical providers, some medical equipment (such as walkers or wheelchairs), as well as some outpatient care and home health care services. Co-payments and deductibles may be required for both Parts A and B.

MEDICARE, PART A:
HOSPITAL INSURANCE

Medicare, Part A covers hospitalization, some services in a skilled nursing facility, hospice care, and some home care. There may be no premiums for Part A insurance if a worker contributed the required 40 quarters to Social Security during their earning years (see *Chapter 2, Finance*). Part A may cover the costs of nursing home stays if:

* after a hospital stay of at least 72 hours the services of a nursing care facility may be required (after three days it is assumed that all hospital care has been extended and the patient is recuperating and needs the services of a health care facility, not a hospital).

* A nursing home stay is required as the result of something diagnosed during a hospital visit. For example, if, during a hospital visit, a broken hip is diagnosed, subsequent nursing home care for physical therapy would be covered.

* Nursing home care would also be covered if a patient is not receiving rehabilitation services but has an ailment or condition that requires skilled nursing supervision.

* The care received at a nursing home must be

SUSAN M. BIGLIONE & MARTHA E. LAISNE

skilled care. (Medicare, Part A does not pay for custodial, non-skilled, or long-term care.)

* The maximum number of days Medicare, Part A, covers at a skilled nursing facility is 100 *per ailment*. While the first 20 days are paid in full by Medicare, the remaining 80 days require a co-payment ($128.00 per day in 2008).

MEDICARE, PART B:

MEDICAL INSURANCE

Part B is optional insurance that helps to pay for some (physician or other care provider) services and products not covered by Part A. The 2008 average monthly premium for **Medicare, Part B** is $96.40.

On the whole, Part B coverage is subject to medical necessity and includes physician and nursing services, X-rays, laboratory and diagnostic tests, flu vaccinations, blood transfusion, renal diaslysis, outpatient hospital services, and some ambulance transport. It also helps with some medical equipment (canes, walkers, wheelchairs, and mobility scooters, for example). Prosthetic devices (artificial limbs and breast prosthesis following mastectomy, a pair of eyeglasses after cataract surgery, and oxygen for home use) are also covered. In 2008, the deductible for Part B services and supplies is $135.00.

Recognizing that neither Part A nor Part B

172

will pay for all medical costs, there are two other components of Medicare: Parts C and D.

MEDICARE, PART C

Medicare, Part C is referred to as "Medicare Advantage." These plans are offered by private insurers. In addition to coverage comparable to Parts A and B, they may offer drug coverage options.

MEDICARE, PART D,
PRESCRIPTION DRUG PLAN

Medicare, Part D prescription drug insurance covers both brand name and generic prescription drugs at participating pharmacies. Anyone enrolled in Medicare, Part A or B, is eligible to enroll in Part D.

Note: A lifetime penalty amount will be added to your monthly Medicare, Part D, premiums if you do not join when you are first eligible. The penalty is 1% of $27.93 (the current year's national average premium) or $0.28 for every full month you were eligible to join and did not. You pay this higher amount as long as you are enrolled in Medicare, although there are exceptions.

Part D benefits are not automatic; to receive them, a Medicare enrollee must enroll in the separate

Prescription Drug plan or a Medicare Advantage plan with prescription drug coverage. These plans are approved and regulated by the Medicare program but administered by private insurers. Part D coverage is not standardized; that is, the insurer decides which drugs (or classes of drugs) they will and will not cover. Since Medicare specifically excludes some drugs, insurers may not request reimbursement for them from Medicare. That means that if you must purchase drugs that are not reimbursed by Medicare, be sure your prescription drug insurance policy covers them.

For people with limited income and resources, these plans may not have a premium. There are three types of private Medicare plans: (1) Medicare Cost plans, (2) Medicare Private Fee-for-Service plans, and (3) Medicare Medical Savings Account plans.

(1) Medicare Cost plans are a type of HMO and work in much the same way as Medicare Advantage plans. With these plans, using out-of-network providers is covered under Part A and co-pays, co-insurance, and deductibles are required. HMOs establish relationships with private doctors who specialize in a particular type of care or are in general practice. These doctors form the HMO network and HMOs only cover care from network doctors. Although they may be less expensive than other plans, patients are limited to using the doctors in the network. When the care of an "out-of-network"

specialist is needed, these plans require that patients get referrals from network doctors. For an extra fee, some plans allow patients to see a specialist without prior approval.

(2) Under a Medicare Private Fee-for-Service plan you may go to any doctor or hospital that accepts the plan's payment. The insurer, rather than Medicare, decides how much it will pay for the services you receive and determines the amount of the co-payment, co-insurance, and deductible.

(3) A Medicare Medical Savings Account is a type of Medicare Advantage plan. To be eligible, you must also have a private high-deductible insurance plan. High-deductible insurance plans require that you meet the annual deductible amount before the Medical Savings Account can be used to pay costs. Another form of Medical Savings Account is one into which Medicare deposits money that you may use to pay health care costs.

Medicare recipients may receive health care services from Medicare's traditional fee-for-service providers or from managed care network plan providers. "Fee-for-service" means that patients may see any physician who participates in Medicare; the physician treats the patient and submits their bill to Medicare for reimbursement.

Medicare costs and benefits are discussed in *Chapter 4, Insurance.*

To apply for Medicare, visit your local Social

Security office or call Social Security at 1–800–772–1213 or apply online at www.ssa.gov.

MEDICAID

Medicaid programs, funded by the state and government, are administered by the state. Based on need, Medicaid helps to pay for the medical care of low-income, older, or disabled people and some other individuals, including those with moderate incomes but high health care expenses. Unlike Medicare, eligibility for Medicaid is based on income and assets. While each state must follow basic eligibility and benefit guidelines, significant details vary among states.

In general, Medicaid covers more nursing home care than does Medicare as well as paying for custodial and skilled care, and most states do not limit the length of time a beneficiary can stay at a nursing home or other care facility. Both Medicare and Medicaid can be a source of funding for long-term home health care, but Medicare covers home health care only if the person is homebound and needs skilled nursing or therapy services.

Medicaid pays health care providers directly. Depending on your state's laws, you may also be required to pay a small part of the cost (a co-payment).

SOCIAL SECURITY BENEFITS

The Social Security program is primarily designed to provide retirement income and to help children of a household in which the primary earner is deceased. Medical benefits offered by the Social Security Administration are limited and designed to help low-income persons with disabilities, blindness, and certain others who qualify. For more information, their website, www.ssa.gov, is very informative and easy to read.

HEALTH SAVINGS ACCOUNTS (HSAS)

A **health savings account** is an individual fund into which you and your employer can contribute for future medical expenses. There is an annual dollar limit on the amount you can contribute and all contributions are tax deductible. Any adult can contribute to an HSA if they:

* have no other medical coverage (except insurance for specific diseases, accidents or injuries and disability, dental, vision, and long-term care are allowed);

* have coverage under an HSA-qualified "high deductible" health plan;

* are not enrolled in Medicare; or

* cannot be claimed as a dependent on someone else's income tax return.

Upon enrolling in Medicare, you may no longer contribute to a health savings account, but you can keep all the money in your account.

You can also grow your account through investments. You may invest the money in the account (in, for example, a mutual fund) and the HSA receives any profits. With an HSA there are three tax savings: your contributions are tax deductible (that is, you can deduct them on your annual income tax returns); investment earnings are tax free; and any withdrawals for qualified medical expenses are tax free.

An HSA is portable; if you change jobs, you can take the HSA with you.

HEALTH REIMBURSEMENT ACCOUNTS (HRAS)

Health reimbursement accounts are also called health reimbursement arrangements. Any size company may offer HRAs to its employees, but only the employer may contribute to the account. Employees pay their own medical expenses and submit claims to the company for reimbursement that are paid from the HRA. There is no limit on the dollar amount of reimbursement claims. When employees leave the company, they may not withdraw any funds from the account because the funds belong to the company, not the employee.

There have been reports that an individual's credit ratings will be linked to HRAs. While the industry has not embraced the idea, now would be the time to get your credit scores sorted out.

POWER OF ATTORNEY FOR HEALTH CARE

Whether you are age 21 or 121, a power of attorney for health care is a wise investment of your time. It allows you to designate someone (a relative or friend, called an "agent") to make on-the-spot medical decisions on your behalf if you cannot.

It is not something we want to think much about in our everyday lives, but a **health care proxy** (as it is sometimes called) has real value. Its value is the peace of mind and assurance of knowing that your wishes regarding medical care will be carried out and is one of the few times in life you have the power to influence how an unexpected event plays out. We don't know when or what extraordinary events will occur, but we can assure that our instructions for care will be respected.

No one should spend their life thinking about what might happen. We have no way of knowing, and we have better things to do than think about something that might never occur. Stock traders "hedge" their bets. They have a plan in place in case a trade tanks and they begin to lose money. The "hedge" is another trade that they think will make enough money to offset a loss. We can use the same strategy for unexpected events. A power of attorney for health care is a way to make sure that in a health emergency, you have responsible, trustworthy people ready and able to step in to make your wishes known.

Don't dismiss this as something "the doctors will handle." They will, but do you want to live with the consequences? Protect yourself. You probably have smoke detectors in your home, an insurance policy on your car, and you use passwords to protect against unauthorized access to your computer; why not assure that you have someone to step in to protect your health care interests?

Finally, don't be put off by its title; *When Life Changes Forever* is all about giving you information, help, and encouragement. After reading this section you should be able to discuss your wishes and create a power of attorney for health care. A simple example is provided in the *Appendix*. You can do this and you should.

Powers of attorney come in three basic forms: durable, nondurable, and springing. Each of these is discussed in *Chapter 4, Legal*. Basically, durable means permanent, that is, once it's signed it will remain in effect until you revoke it or die. Nondurable means that it is temporary and remains in effect for only as long as specified in its terms and may be revoked at any time. The springing form becomes effective only when some event (or events), that you specify, occurs.

When you are admitted to a hospital, care facility, or visit your physician, you may be asked for or encouraged to sign a power of attorney for health care. In most such situations it will be a durable power of attorney. Why? Since it is permanent, it is the easiest type of power of attorney for the hospital, care facility, or physician to deal with; they simply file it away for future reference and presume that you will not change your mind or your agent and won't go through the trouble of revoking it.

What are your options? Nondurable and springing powers of attorney. With a nondurable power of attorney you can limit your agent's time commitment to only the current hospital visit; when you are discharged from the hospital, the power of attorney ends. Similarly, with a springing power of attorney for health care, if, for example, during your visit to the hospital, you are diagnosed with a terminal illness or condition, a springing power of attorney could become effective when some event happens (you can no longer communicate your wishes or fall into a coma or vegetative state). For example, you may designate that the event that triggers a springing power of attorney is that two doctors, one of whom you may name, agree with that diagnosis. That is, two doctors, one of whom may be your personal physician, are asked their opinions; if they both agree that it is unlikely that you will recover, this type of power of attorney springs into effect. Or, if the doctors believe that you will recover, and you can communicate your wishes for treatment, the springing power of attorney will not become effective. You decide what events trigger a springing power of attorney.

Let's repeat our mantra: "I am the customer, I make the decisions. You are the service provider, provide the service I want." When you need medical assistance for any reason, there are serious risks involved. No power of attorney will cover all situations and, for all practical purposes, a power of attorney for health care is as much for the legal protection of the hospital, care facility, or physician as it is for you. Providing a power of attorney for health care is, in most states, not a law but a rule established by the hospital, health care facility, or physician to prevent law suits. If you would prefer to use a nondurable or springing power of attorney, that's your choice. Life changes, and what is appropriate now may not be in the future when the **durable power of attorney** for **health care** will still be on file with your care provider (or you have forgotten to revoke it by notifying them in writing and retrieved the old copy). Moreover, if the agent named in a durable power of attorney is absent or no longer available, the power of attorney is useless, will not be considered, and you are left with no reliable support.

In any case, however, any power of attorney for health care only becomes effective when you are no longer able to give or withdraw informed consent regarding your care. As long as you can make and communicate reasonable decisions, your wishes are law.

Sometimes people use the terms "power of attorney for health care" and "living will" interchangeably, but there is a difference. A power of attorney names an agent to represent you. A living will only states your wishes concerning what medical treatment(s) you do or do not want (see below). You may combine the characteristics of a power of attorney and a living will. See *Living Will* below.

Your agent may discuss your medical situation with doctors and other medical personnel to make sure you are receiving the kind of care you want and review your medical records but cannot make decisions on financial matters. Without a power of attorney for health care, because of patient confidentiality, discussions on these matters are restricted to spouse and next-of-kin.

Before your agent can make any responsible decisions, they must know your wishes. Your agent expresses your wishes and sees to it that others respect them. Discuss your choices clearly and in detail to be sure they have a complete understanding. We read all the time about families disagreeing on medical care and dragging their dispute through court. It is unnecessary, time consuming, expensive, and may even be painful.

Many hospitals and health care facilities request copies of your power of attorney for health care or living will at admission. If you have not completed either of them, they will provide a blank one. At admission or lying on a gurney is hardly the time for calm, rational thought.

Caution: Be absolutely sure you know the hospital policy with regard to care after the terms of a power of attorney for healthcare are accepted. That is, if life-sustaining treatment is not to be administered or is withdrawn, it may be the hospital's policy to discharge the patient.

Never sign any form unless and until you have read it and it accurately reflects your wishes. An improperly completed document is invalid. Your agent should have several originals and keep copies in the *Medical* folder of your *Life File*. If you regularly visit a medical facility or doctor, they should have a copy on file.

LIVING WILL

After thousands of years of trying, no one has yet been able to predict the future, and we can confidently predict that in the future no one will. Although some workers have been known to "schedule" sick days, we can only wonder about our fate on earth. Some people feel that accidents, illness, and our eventual demise are too difficult or depressing to dwell on. They're right; we shouldn't dwell on them, but we should prepare for them.

One of the ways to do that is by creating a living will. A **living will** is a person's instructions about how they wish to be treated when they can no longer tell anyone what they want. It is a legal document that defines how they wish to cope with accidents or illnesses that medical science cannot fix. It expresses their wishes about care when they are in a coma (or vegetative state), are terminally ill (with no expectation of recovery), and when death is imminent.

As long as you are able to communicate your wishes, a living will will not become effective. Living wills and health care powers of attorney only become effective when you no longer have the ability to give informed consent to receive medical treatments or to request that they not be administered or request that they be withdrawn.

It is your basic right to control decisions made about your medical care. It is your basic responsibility to be clear about your desires and not leave these extreme and heartrending decisions to anyone else at a time when emotions can be so fragile.

As the example in the *Appendix* shows, a living will has a list of questions and space to express your personal preferences. Make clear, consistent choices; inconsistent or contradictory choices will not accomplish your goals. It will do no good, and perhaps some harm, to add contingencies and requirements that cannot be honored. If a living will cannot be honored, it will be ignored.

Some of the terms found in a living include "extreme" (or sometimes "extraordinary") means. **Extreme means** may include the use of breathing tubes (respirators) or other invasive means to support or replace a vital bodily function that is no longer working. **"Artificial means"** refers to food and water, feeding tubes, or other invasive means of providing nutrition.

If a medical condition is terminal and incurable or if a person is in a persistent vegetative state or irreversible coma, a living will may be the only way to inform medical personnel of what treatment to administer, not administer, or withdraw. A living will is consulted only after all generally expected medical treatments have failed. In it you express your wishes about life-sustaining medical procedures: that you do (or do not) wish to receive life support services; or that you do (or do not) wish to have life support systems removed when either you are terminally and incurably ill and/or are diagnosed as being in a persistent vegetative state.

To prepare a valid living will, in most states, you must be a mentally competent adult (usually 18 years old) able to comprehend, make, and communicate your decisions at the time the living will is created. A living will must contain some specific statements about your intentions. These required statements vary from state to state, but the language below is representative.

* You must state that you do, or do not, want the use of extreme or artificial means to supply water and nutrition to preserve life, particularly if your condition is terminal and incurable or if you are in a coma or persistent vegetative state.

* You must state that you understand that your living will allows the doctor to withhold or stop extreme or artificial medical treatments.

* You must sign the document in the presence of two qualified witnesses and the document must be notarized.

Caution: Be absolutely sure you know the hospital policy with regard to care after the terms of a living will are accepted. That is, if life-sustaining treatment is not to be administered or is withdrawn, it may be the hospital's policy to discharge the patient.

These are life and death issues; do not make them without professional help.

AGENTS AND WITNESSES

Qualified witnesses to your living will are important. Most witnesses to legal documents are there so that if anyone asks later, they can truthfully say that they watched someone sign their name. Simple as that. With a living will, the rules are a little different. Two witnesses (in some states, three) are required to sign a living will in the presence of a notary public. So that it cannot be questioned or implied later that a witness had an interest in prematurely shipping anyone off to Valhalla, certain persons are excluded. At least one witness may *not* be: (1) related to you or your spouse; (2) stand to inherit any of your estate; (3) have a claim against you or your estate; or (4) be your doctor, a relative of your doctor, your doctor's employee, or a paid employee of the hospital or other care facility such as a nursing home, or group care facility at which you are a resident or patient.

You may revoke a living will at any time. If you generate a new living will, be sure to add a statement revoking all others. Each state has its own rules and you need to use a format that adheres to your state law. Most hospitals, private physicians, or medical care facilities have blank forms and their staff will be glad to discuss your options. To assure that your living will complies with state law, ask for a couple of blank copies from your physician or local hospital (the Nursing Supervisor's office should have them).

Use one for your notes and after you've thought it through, write your wishes on the other before taking it to an attorney for review, to have it notarized, witnessed, and signed.

As previously mentioned, the characteristics of a power of attorney for health care and a living will may be combined. To do so, you may add language to your living will that designates an agent, who will have the same responsibilities as outlined in a power of attorney. The example in the *Appendix* displays this option.

Keep a couple of completed copies in your **Life File**. If you've named an agent, they should have a couple of originals, and your attorney should keep a copy on file.

CHAPTER 4: *Insurance*

DECIPHERING THE CODES

For almost every lifestyle and circumstance there's an insurance policy out there just waiting for a signature, and almost anything imaginable can be insured; buildings, art, pets, jewelry, body parts, and there are even policies that insure personal behavior. If you own it, drive it, use, or wear it, someone will insure it, as they have for 1,500 years since the Romans and Greeks insured families and paid funeral expenses for the members of guilds called "Benevolent Societies."

Another way to protect ourselves is with the law. The Declaration of **Homestead Exemption** is available in most but not every state; the following is excerpted from the Massachusetts Registry of Deeds (www. mass.gov/legis/laws/mgl/188–1.htm accessed 2/4/07):

> Homestead is a type of protection for a person's residence, in the form of a document called a Declaration of Estate of Homestead. The form is filed at the Registry of Deeds in the county where the property is located…It allows Massachusetts homeowners to protect their property up to five

hundred thousand dollars ($500,000) of the value per residence, per family…The real property or manufactured home which serves as an individual's principal residence upon filing a declaration of Homestead, shall be protected against subsequent attachment, levy on execution and sale to satisfy debts to the extent of five hundred thousand dollars ($500,000) per residence, per family.

The Declaration of Homestead Exemption is a form you file with your county recorder's office that states your right to a homestead exemption. In most states this is automatic. Homestead exemption laws protect your home in a bankruptcy. If you live in a state that has Homestead exemption laws, go to their website or contact your local County Clerk for assistance.

HOMEOWNERS AND RENTERS INSURANCE

A homeowners or renters policy generally protects the contents of your home, condo, or apartment against fire, windstorm, hurricane, hail, theft, personal liability, medical payments to others; and, of course, policies have exceptions and limitations. It may also cover the cost of additional living expenses if you must leave your residence, and some provide replacement costs.

There are many resources you can check and many ways to save. Contact your state insurance department or the Consumer Action Website (www.consumeraction.gov, accessed 3/8/07), which has an informative 2007 Consumer Action Handbook and consumer reports for information to help you choose a policy that meets your needs.

Don't consider price alone; the insurer you select should offer a fair price and deliver the quality of service you demand; also ask what they can do to lower your costs.

To check the financial stability of the companies you are considering, check with rating services such as A.M. Best (www.ambest.com) or consult consumer-reporting publications. When you've narrowed the field to three, get price quotes.

Insurance Deductibles. **Deductibles** are amounts you pay out of pocket before the insurer will begin reimbursement; that is, you must first pay the entire deductible amount before the insurer will start paying any charges. It is usually an annual amount, and some plans have both individual and family deductibles. Typically, deductibles are $100, $250, or $500. A "high deductible" would be $1,000 or more.

The higher the deductible, the more you can save on premiums. Most insurers recommend a $500 deductible, but if you can raise the deductible to $1,000, you may save as much as 25% on premiums. If you live in a disaster-prone area (such as windstorm, hail, or earthquake), there may be separate deductibles for these expected events.

Insurance Discounts. Finding out what steps you can take to make your home more disaster resistant, and taking them may save on premiums. Discounts (up to 5%) may be achieved by installing smoke and carbon monoxide detectors, burglar alarms, or dead-bolt locks. If you're at least 55 years old and retired, you may qualify for a 10% discount. Long-term (3–5 years) policyholders may receive a 5% discount and a 10% discount for staying with the company for six or more years. Some employers and professional associations administer group insurance programs that offer lower premiums than elsewhere.

Review your policy every year to be sure it covers any major purchases or additions to your home, and don't spend money for coverage you don't need. If you have riders for expensive items that are no longer worth their original price (they have "depreciated"—lost value over time), cancel the rider and pocket the money. A **rider** provides coverage for specific items not covered under a policy. It is an addition to the policy, and there is an extra premium for each rider. For items with relatively stable values or that increase in value, jewelry, for example, check that you are neither underinsured or overinsured.

Renters policies, or "contents" policies, cover the contents of the unit in which the policyholder lives. A landowner or landlord's insurance does not cover renters and their personal belongings. The landlord's insurance only protects the structure and the landlord's personal property, not a tenant's property and/or personal belongings, and many landlords require renters to carry insurance on their belongings. If windows, walls, or carpeting are damaged by the renter, the renter or their insurance must pay for the damages.

HEALTH AND LIFE POLICIES

This is not the easiest sledding, so crank up the "I'm taking charge" meter to 11 and climb aboard.

In its simplest form, health and life insurance policies are contracts with insurers that promise to provide health benefit coverage and/or, in an odd interpretation, life policies provide your beneficiaries with an amount of money upon your death.

Policies may be purchased from an insurance broker or insurance agent, through your employer, and some professional or fraternal associations. Payments (called **premiums**) are generally based on your age, gender, occupation, credit rating, medical history, the total dollar amount of the policy, and some policies require a qualifying medical exam.

Most, if not all health policies require deductibles and **co-payments** or **co-insurance**, that are payments shared by you and the service provider at the time care is provided.

Before you tuck a policy away in your *Life File*, check the beneficiary(ies). A **beneficiary** is the person or entity you name to receive the death benefit. You can name one, two, or more persons, a trust, a charity, or a funeral home (but you should not name an individual at a charity or funeral home). If you don't name a beneficiary, the benefit is paid to your estate.

All health policies have "lifetime maximum benefits" and "maximum policy benefit amounts." **Lifetime maximum benefits** refer to the benefits that will be paid over the life of the policy. If your health policy has a lifetime maximum amount of $30,000 and the total cost of your first hospital visit under this policy is $31,000, you have exceeded the policy's lifetime maximum and the policy ends (and you owe the hospital $1,000). **Policy maximum benefits** refer to individual medical procedures or equipment. If the policy indicates that it will reimburse for one radiology session and you need two sessions, you will have to pay for one of them.

It is important to know these maximums and how much you have used. If you have not received this information from your insurer, request it. A common problem is that notoriously incorrect hospital charges reported to insurers reduce your maximum benefits. Since hospital billing departments have a 10%-12% error rate, if you are charged $1,020.00 for an "oral hygiene assembly," you can point out to the hospital Billing Manager that the price seems a little high for a toothbrush and save $1,018.00 in insurance benefits for more important medical issues.

You should have a basic understanding of the terms of your policy. Policies bought years ago may not be suitable today. Contact your insurance agent and ask for an explanation and, if appropriate, discuss upgrading. Take notes on your conversation and attach them to the policy filed in your *Life File*.

If you are looking for an agent, choose someone who represents several companies and ask them for side-by-side comparisons of the best prices. Most life insurance companies have 10–20 different prices, for fairly similar policies, and several health ratings and an agent representing several companies will have all the information available. Among other things, a health rating is a ranking used by insurance companies that qualifies potential policyowners on their present health, medical history, family medical history, driving record, and occupation, and affects the premiums offered.

If you are in good health, premiums on older policies may have come down, but the insurance company has no obligation to advise you of lower rates; check with your agent. Most insurers also offer optional coverage (riders) for children, return of premium (see below), disability, accidental death, and many other events that need to be considered carefully. Some industry analysts feel that riders are profitable for insurers because they either cover events that rarely occur or their terms are so limited that it is unlikely that the benefit will ever be paid. Read the policy carefully.

Although the terms of personal insurance policies vary widely, as we will see, there are two basic types: **term life** or **permanent life** also called "whole" or "universal" life. A term life policy provides a pre-set benefit amount to beneficiaries if you die during the term stated in the policy. If you purchase a 10-year term policy and outlive it, the policy lapses. You may have the option to renew it for the same number of years as the original policy; in this example, an additional ten years. Premiums generally increase as you age and the risk of death increases.

Whole life insurance provides coverage for a policy-owner's entire life. Premiums are fixed amounts.

A **variable life** policy is a type of whole life insurance for which some or all of the premiums are invested by the insurer and the amount of the death benefit depends on the performance of the investments.

Universal life insurance is also a type of whole life and premiums, benefits, and benefits payment schedules are variable, not fixed. See the *Glossary*.

A **variable universal life** plan, also under the whole-life umbrella, provides greater flexibility and risk. Premiums are variable, as are benefit payments and payment schedules. The risk is in how premiums are invested; that is, premiums are invested in stocks rather than more stable vehicles such as Treasuries (see *Chapter 2, Finance*).

File all policies and your notes in your *Life File*.

Health care and disability insurance coverage are no longer luxuries for most people. Employer group plans enroll so many souls (a quaint industry reference) that premiums for employer-sponsored plans are slightly more expensive than for privately purchased policies.

Following are the general categories of health insurance policies.

Basic insurance plans   cover hospitalization and related charges.

Medical and **surgical insurance plans** cover physicians services, **"inpatient"** (when a person is admitted to a hospital or clinic and is required to stay overnight), and **"outpatient"** (when a person is admitted to a hospital or clinic but does not stay overnight) service charges and certain other charges (such as radiology, imaging, and laboratory tests) depending on the policy.

Major medical or **catastrophic plans**   cover only specific illness or injury.

Comprehensive major medical plans   cover all or most of the above under one plan.

Blue Cross Blue Shield "the Blues" are a national federation of not-for-profit service organizations that contract with individual hospitals (Blue

Cross) and physicians (Blue Shield) to provide prepaid health care. These policies usually pay a flat amount for a semi-private hospital room or nursing services, rather than paying individual charges.

Hospital indemnity plans pay a specified, fixed-dollar amount per day for hospitalization, no matter what the actual charges are and what other insurance coverage the insured has.

Specified disease plans pay a fixed, flat amount for each day of hospitalization for a specific condition or disease.

Hospital indemnity and specified disease plans are intended to supplement other hospitalization coverage.

Medicare private fee-for-service plan Private insurance plans that accept Medicare participants. Plan members are free to use any Medicare-participating doctor or medical facility. The insurer, rather than Medicare, decides how much and for what services it will reimburse, and, consequently, premiums may be high. They usually cover benefits not included in the basic Medicare plans.

COBRA: Comprehensive Omnibus Budget Reconciliation Act of 1989. Most of us won't recognize the name, but **COBRA** is an important part of our health care rights for two reasons. First, it guarantees continued group coverage during the time between when an individual leaves one employer's group plan and joins another. It also guarantees that premiums during the COBRA period (while you're transferring from one employer plan to another) remain the same as the group rates in force before the COBRA period began. And, second, it guarantees minimum, life-sustaining treatment and stabilization procedures for anyone in emergency care whether or not they have insurance.

Federal law requires that employers notify employees of events (termination, reduction of work hours, or other circumstances) that trigger an employee's COBRA rights. COBRA gives the unemployed and covered family members the right to retain and/or continue the group coverage rates they had when they were employed until they can enroll in another group plan or change their coverage to a private plan. In certain situations, a retired employee, their spouse, and dependent children may be qualified beneficiaries.

Under COBRA, coverage is continued for a period beyond employment (18, 29, or 36 months). The COBRA coverage period may not be extended, though some states offer extensions to people who can't find insurance elsewhere. You may convert to a private policy or transfer to a new employer's plan any time during the COBRA continuation period.

Not all employers are subject to COBRA and

may offer their own conversion plans to continue coverage. The cost of COBRA coverage is 100% of the group plan premium plus 2%, but it may be your best bet since you benefit from employer group rates during the COBRA period.

MEDICARE COVERAGE

Medicare is the primary insurer for Americans 65 years old or older. You qualify for Medicare benefits based on your own or your spouse's employment record. For those also covered by private insurance, Medicare pays medical bills first before other insurance plans begin to pay reimbursements. Medicare coverage has four parts: A, B, C, and D.

Medicare, Part A, hospital fee-for-service, covers costs for medically necessary inpatient services supplied at a hospital (a semi-private room and meals, general nursing and services such as some drugs, lab tests, X-rays, chemotherapy, and operating-room services). "Medically necessary" means any services needed for the diagnosis and treatment of a medical condition that meets accepted standards of medical practice. You may receive Medicare benefits for hospice care or while at a skilled nursing facility. Also covered is 100% of **home health care** and 80% of the cost of approved medical equipment. Part A benefits are financed through the Social Security (FICA) tax paid by employers and employees, so there are no premiums for qualified Medicare, Part A, recipients.

Medicare, Part B, broadly defines the coverage for the services of physicians and surgeons and certain other medical services and supplies at a hospital, physician's office, or nursing home. Reimbursement may include such items as X-rays, laboratory tests, ambulance services, cardiac rehabilitation programs, and medical equipment. Part B coverage is optional for a monthly premium and available to anyone enrolled in Part A. Generally, Medicare covers 80% of Part B expenses, but Part B does not cover expenses for prescription drugs (although it does pay for drugs administered in a hospital), routine physical exams, dental bills, vision or hearing tests. People over 65 or disabled may purchase both Parts A and B if they are not automatically eligible for Part A.

Medicare, Part C, is referred to as "Medicare Advantage." These plans are offered by private insurers. In addition to coverage comparable to Parts A and B, they may offer drug coverage options.

Medicare, Part D, Prescription Drug plans are offered by private insurers and cover both brand name and generic prescription drugs at participating pharmacies. Anyone enrolled in Medicare, Part A or B, is eligible to enroll in Part D. Premiums vary depending on the plan.

See also *Medicare* in *Chapter 3.*

MEDICARE COVERAGE COSTS

Most people do not pay a monthly premium for Medicare, Part A, because they (or their spouse) contributed to the FICA fund during their working years. To receive Medicare benefits without paying a premium, you must have 40 or more quarters of Medicare-covered employment in the same way as you qualify for Social Security benefits (see *What is Social Security?* in *Chapter 2, Finance*). If you have not contributed for the required 40 quarters, Medicare, Part A, may be purchased for a 2008 monthly premium of up to $423.00 depending on the number of quarters earned.

The average 2008 monthly premium for Medicare, Part, B, is $96.40; however, if your income is greater than $82,000 (for an individual) and $164,000 (for a married couple), premiums will be higher and are scaled up.

You may arrange to have your Medicare premiums automatically deducted from your Social Security check.

The table below is reproduced from Medicare's website (www.medicare.gov, accessed 2/10/08).

You Pay	If Your Yearly Income Is
	Single
$93.50	$80,000 or less
$105.80	$80,001-$100,000
$124.40	$100,001-$150,000
$142.90	$150,001-$200,000
$161.40	Above $200,000

You Pay	If Your Yearly Income Is
	Married
$93.50	$160,000 or less
$105.80	$160,001-$200,000
$124.40	$200,001-$300,000
$142.90	$300,001-$400,000
$161.40	Above $400,000

You Pay	If You are Married but you File a Separate Tax Return from your Spouse and Your Yearly Income is
$93.50	Under $80,000 or less

You Pay	If You are Married but you File a Separate Tax Return from your Spouse and Your Yearly Income is
$142.90	$80,001 - $120,000
$161.40	Above $120,000

The costs of Parts C and D plans depend on the insurer.

DEDUCTIBLES AND CO-PAYMENTS

To understand deductibles and co-payments, you must first understand **"benefit periods"**. Benefit periods have a definite beginning and end, and Medicare benefits, and the co-payments required, are based on these strictly defined periods of time. For Part A (hospital) benefits, the benefit period begins when you first enter a hospital and ends 60 (consecutive) days after all inpatient care was provided.

> Simple example: You entered a hospital on January 1. Your hospital visit lasted two weeks and you did not return to the hospital for follow-up care *for the same condition*. The entire benefit period would begin on January 1, go through January 14, and end 60 days after January 14 (or about March 16). The same time frame applies to skilled nursing care.

From this example, you have used one Medicare benefit period. For each benefit period, Medicare pays all covered costs except the $1,024 deductible for days 1–60 of hospitalization and any co-payment required for any days beyond day 61 (see below). If you return to the hospital after March 16, a new benefit period begins. There is no limit to the number of benefit periods covered by Part A during your lifetime.

There are some restrictions, of course. Coverage for one hospital visit is limited to 90 days during one benefit period. During those ninety days, after the deductible has been paid, days 1 through 60 are covered by Medicare, Part A. For each of days 61 to 90 a co-payment is required, as follows.

Part A—For each 2008 benefit period, a beneficiary will pay:

* A $1,024 deductible for days 1–60 of a hospital stay.

* For each day between day 61 and day 90, the co-payment is $256.

* For hospitalization longer than 90 days, there are payment options.

* For each day between day 91 and day 150, the co-payment is $512, as part of your limited Lifetime Reserve Days.

In all Medicare beneficiaries' lifetimes, Medicare has "reserved" 60 days over and above what the basic Medicare, Part A, policy offers that may be used at any time, and during which basic Medicare, Part A, benefits and policies apply. These reserve days are a nonrenewable resource; that is, if you use some of the days, they are not replaced and you have fewer reserve days left. While you can use reserve days as often as you need them, there are only 60 reserve days available during your lifetime. (Medigap policies, see below, often contain a benefit for 365 hospital days during your lifetime.)

* For day 91 through day 150, pay all costs out of pocket or use Medigap insurance (see below) to cover some or all costs.

Using the services of a skilled nursing facility under Medicare, Part A requires payment of an annual deductible and a $128.00 per day co-payment for days 21 through 100 for each 2008 benefit period.

For Part B (medical) benefits, first the annual 2008 deductible of $135.00 is required, then co-payments for covered services and co-insurance of 20% of the Medicare-approved amounts of all equipment covered by Part B.

For Parts C and D, deductible and co-payment, fees vary by plan.

MEDIGAP POLICIES

Since Medicare doesn't pay for everything, there are "gaps" in its coverage. Medicare Supplemental Insurance policies, also known as **Medigap policies** can help with costs that Medicare does not cover. There are two important features of some Medigap policies: the number of days of hospitalization coverage defined in the terms of the policy and deductibles and co-payments benefits. Ordinarily, deductibles, and co-payments are out-of-pocket expenses; as part of their benefits, some Medigap policies offer to cover these expenses.

The more gaps you want to fill, the more expensive the policy will be. There are dozens of types of Medigap policies available, and while these policies are not government sponsored, the terms and benefits offered are regulated by the government. When reviewing these policies, think about which gaps you'll need to fill as well as the cost of each policy. Also consider health status, expected needs, and benefit restrictions (on, for example, chronic or pre-existing conditions and drugs).

All Medigap policies must contain the basic Medicare benefits. That is, all policies include coverage of:

* Medicare, Part A, co-payment ($256 per day) for

days 61 through 90 of a hospital stay (in each Medicare benefit period);

* Medicare, Part A, co-payment ($512 per day) for days 91 through 150 of a hospital stay (for each lifetime reserve day);

* After all Medicare, Part A, benefits are exhausted, coverage of 100% of Medicare-eligible hospital expenses;

* A lifetime maximum of at least 60 days of additional inpatient hospital care;

* Coverage for the reasonable cost of the first three pints of blood (or equivalent of packed red blood cells) per year (unless the blood is replaced); and

* Coverage for Part B services after the $135 annual deductible is met.

Other policies may include such coverage items as: hospital deductible coverage, skilled nursing home co-payment coverage, coverage for annual deductibles for doctors' services, at-home care, foreign travel emergency care (although Part A has some limited coverage), preventive care costs, and prescription drug costs.

The best time to sign up for Medigap insurance is within six months of enrolling in Medicare, Part B. Within that time, your application must be accepted and all pre-existing medical conditions will be covered. After six months your application can be refused for reasons of age, pre-existing illness, or acceptance may rely on a medical exam that you may be less likely to pass.

MEDICAID

Although some people may qualify for both Medicare and Medicaid, they are not the same. Medicaid is designed for the low income or medically needy, and although it is sponsored by both federal and state governments, it is administered by individual states. Eligibility requirements differ from state to state but generally include financial need and consideration of recipients under the age of 21 or over 65 or who are blind or disabled. When considering income or current financial eligibility, all states exempt a person's home but include other assets, including savings. Medicaid reimbursements are paid directly to service providers and, in general, include:

* Inpatient, outpatient hospital services, and physician services

* Prenatal care

* Vaccines for children

* Nursing facility services for persons aged 21 or older

* Family planning services and supplies

* Rural health clinic services

* Home health care for persons eligible for skilled-nursing service

* Laboratory and X-ray services

* Pediatric and family nurse practitioner services

* Nurse-midwife services

* Early and periodic screening, diagnostic, and treatment for children under age 21

LONG-TERM CARE INSURANCE

As discussed in *Chapter 3, Medical,* in old age or disability, there are many resources available: home health services, adult daycare centers, assisted-living facilities, and nursing homes. For most people, however, paying for these services is the problem. One answer may be **long-term care insurance** that covers nursing homes charges or other forms of long-term care.

Long-term care benefit policies do not rely only on age. Policies are generally expensive but provide extended benefits for nursing home care or rehabilitation. Payments for medical costs and expenses are made directly to the service provider once conventional health coverage is exhausted.

According to recent surveys, the annual cost of nursing home care begins at about $35,000, none of which is covered by Medicare. According to some in-the-know, a 40-year-old hoping to retire at age 55 would need to save $650 a month for their health care needs alone (to be used between the ages of 55 and 80).

Long-term care policies are expensive and risky. Benefits may cover only a portion of expenses. If premiums increase you risk dropping the policy and losing your entire investment. You may have too many medical issues to qualify for coverage. And if you plan to use the policy 20 or 30 years from now, will the insurer still be in business?

The grade for such policies, so far, would be a "C." Premium rates have doubled or increased very dramatically. One in four 65-year-olds flunk the physical exam, and by age 70 one in three can't pass. Deductibles, in the form of elimination periods, 20, 30, 60, 90, or 100 days when you must pay out of your own pocket, are high.

What to do? As always, the answer is: research, research, research. To get started, following are some topics you may wish to investigate.

Although salespeople want you to buy a policy at age 40, the coverage may not exist twenty years in the future when you need it. New medical technologies and health care systems will no doubt be developed that won't remotely resemble the kind of care you would expect to receive today compared to twenty years in the future but that you will pay premiums

WHEN LIFE CHANGES FOREVER

for over twenty years. (Twenty years ago, there were no long-term care policies.) Consider waiting until you are age 55 or 60 if you have a chronic condition that could incapacitate you over time. Since the average age of an adult entering nursing home care is in the eighties, begin to assess your needs at about age 60 and wait until age 65 to buy. If you buy after age 70 the policy will be more expensive or you may not pass the medical test to qualify.

When buying anything for future use, especially in the very distant future, you'll want to be sure that it will be there when you are. Shop around for a very strong company. A.M. Best (www.ambest.com) rates insurers.

One of the points to consider when shopping for long-term care is assistance with one of the five activities of daily living (bathing, eating, dressing, toileting, and walking). Most long-term care insurance policies require that the insured person be able to perform three or four of these functions without assistance. All of them are, of course, important, but from the standpoint of patient assistance it is important that bathing be one of the covered benefits, particularly if a person is (or can be expected to be) confined to bed for long periods of time. It is estimated that 94% of nursing home residents need help with bathing, so be sure your policy covers it.

Spousal discounts may be available. Some

insurers offer a discount if both a husband and wife purchase life insurance at the same time. Each year the discount is deducted from the total cost of both policies.

Look for policies that cover assisted-living care as well as nursing home care. Coverage can vary between 50% and more than 100% on the rates charged by nursing homes and assisted living facilities, and assisted living is becoming more widely used. Be careful how the policy qualifies any facility for professional (licensed) or informal (unlicensed) care. Some insurers specify, among other things, that staff members at nursing care facilities be on the premises 24 hours a day, a doctor on call, or that the facility is able to supervise medications.

Some policies offer a rider for home or community care; others offer specific benefits for any qualified setting. The home care benefit should include adult daycare, hospice services, and respite care.

Does the policy pay for needed home modifications (wheelchair ramps or shower safety grips)?

Make sure the policy cannot be canceled based on poor health.

Skilled, intermediate, and custodial care in the home or elsewhere gives the patient the option of staying home and receiving care, or receiving all levels of care at a nursing home or assisted living facility. Each policy is different; check these options before committing to a plan.

Check the waiting (or elimination) period, which should be no longer than three months and be a one-time requirement. If the waiting period begins on the first day that care is received, the insurer will only begin reimbursement 20, 30, 60, 90, or 100 days later, according to the terms of the policy. A twist is to reset the waiting period when a patient moves from one care situation to another. If the waiting period began with home care and the patient is moved to an assisted living facility or nursing home and the waiting period is reset to zero, you would have to pay out of pocket for another 20, 30, etc., days at the new facility at a cost of many thousands of dollars. Forty percent of nursing home and assisted living residents have previously received home care. Make sure the elimination period is a one-time requirement.

Pass up any policy that specifies that hospitalization is required before benefits begin.

Many patients receive a variety of care services each day. Make sure that all anticipated care is taken into consideration.

Call several local nursing homes or assisted living facilities to make sure that the policy you intend to purchase will at very least cover their current charges. If you purchase a long-term policy today, you can expect an annual 5% increase in charges. Calculate what you think you will need based on the services you anticipate receiving and a 5% inflation rate for each year before you expect to receive benefits. Or an inflation rate protection option may be contained in the basic policy. Not all insurers offer this inflation option and it is expensive. In addition, make sure the inflation rate protection specified in the policy is sensible; 2% or 3% is wholly inadequate when prices are rising by 13% a year in the health care industry.

When you purchase an indemnity or per diem (Latin for "for each day") plan, you will be asked to select from a range of daily benefit options that you think will cover your needs twenty or thirty years in the future. The amount the insurer will pay in the future for full daily nursing home care depends on the selections you make now, and they will pay that daily amount regardless of actual charges. A truly absurd claim is that you will be able to keep any surplus (between what the policy will pay in the future and what actual future costs are). Given inflation and the cost of medications today, is it reasonable to think that there will ever be a surplus? Not. And remember, no policy is going to pay more than its specified life-time maximum. Eventually, the policy will stop paying when you reach its dollar maximum—save the surplus for then.

Ninety percent of nursing home residents over age 65 stay less than five years with an average stay being two-and-a-half years. Consider, however, with ever more Baby Boomers entering retirement in far fitter physical shape than any previous generation, these averages will increase dramatically very soon. A four-year (or longer) plan with a 30-day elimination period may be right for you. The longer the term of coverage, of course, the higher the annual premium. Policies with 90-day elimination periods are about 15% less expensive a year than others; but run the numbers: with daily rates hovering around $200 a day today, and a 5% annual inflation rate, twenty years from now those 90 days could conservatively cost in the neighborhood of $45,000 out of pocket.

There are other precautions you may be able to take when contemplating purchasing a long-term policy.

Nonforfeiture clause. If you have to cancel your policy, you can get back the money you paid by adding a nonforfeiture clause. You can claim only as much as you paid in and nothing for inflation protection. It's expensive to add this clause (about 30% of premiums).

Tax-qualified plans. To be tax deductible, medical expenses must be 7.5% of your adjusted gross income. Tax-qualified policy premiums that meet the 7.5% federal standard, allow you to deduct annual premiums (if they meet or exceed 7.5% of your adjusted gross income).

LONG-TERM DISABILITY POLICIES

Long-term **disability insurance** benefits are intended to replace lost income during an expected or normal work career. Fixed dollar amounts are paid periodically to cover loss of income during an extended illness or disability. Benefits stop at a certain age (usually retirement age, 65) or after a certain number of years. The "number of years" is usually equal to the years a person would have worked if they had not become disabled.

Many states allow insurance providers to disclaim (deny) paying benefits on claims that can (or will) be paid by other sources. Some state laws allow insurers to reduce the amount paid on a claim or to recover payments they made that the insured later receives as the result of a lawsuit.

Underinsured or Uninsured?

What can you do if you are uninsured, underinsured, or burdened by the high cost of insurance?

Contact professional or alumni associations you belong to (or could join) to find out if they offer group rates (at lower premiums than privately purchased policies).

Start a part-time, one-person consultancy business. What you do or the money you do, or do not, make doesn't matter, but in some states you can apply for "group of one" insurance to obtain group rates.

Your state may offer extended COBRA eligibility and high-risk pools for people who can't find insurance elsewhere. Contact your state insurance department or check Healthinsuranceinfo.net's *Consumer Guides for Getting and Keeping Health Insurance* at www. iowapublichealth.org (accessed 3/10/07).

If those options don't pan out, shop for individual coverage. Contact a local broker who will price policies for you and consider less-comprehensive coverage, increasing the deductible or accepting limits on prescription drug benefits.

No matter what kind of insurance you have, it is as important to know what the insurer has paid under that policy as it is to know what they will and will not pay. Hospitals have a dismal billing track record with a national average error rate of about 10%—representing billions of dollars annually. This is mostly due to simple errors when assigning code numbers from an incredibly complex coding system. Sometimes, however, it's not: $12 for a "mucus recovery system" (a box of tissues) should be brought to the attention of the hospital Billing Manager.

The reason this is so important is because it affects the lifetime maximum of your insurance. If you are overcharged and are later diagnosed with an expensive illness, you may have less insurance than you think. Your credit rating may also be at risk. Health Maintenance Organizations and other managed care plans may turn overdue accounts over to collection agencies and file nonpayment information with credit reporting bureaus in as few as thirty days.

Always get an itemized list of any costs from

the hospital billing department. Question anything that doesn't seem right. There is help available; the Medical Billing Advocates of America (www.billad-vocates.com) and others can help decipher bills. Medical Billing Advocates of America charges a fee, but compared to what you could save now for later, it may be a small price to pay. Never pay your bill before leaving the hospital; you must be allowed time to review it, and hospitals cannot demand immediate payment before you have had a chance to look it over.

Reject any bill that contains terms like "lab fees" or "miscellaneous fees." Demand an itemization. If you don't get satisfaction from the billing department, contact the hospital administrator pronto.

Make sure all the information in the insurance policy section called "declarations" (that lists covered family members) is accurate; errors (for example, an incorrect Social Security number) can trigger a rejection of benefits.

The "exceptions and exclusions" section of a policy tells you which pre-existing illnesses or experimental procedures your plan excludes or limits.

If you are having elective surgery, ask your doctor what the procedure will cost. The doctor's office can call the insurer to find out what will be covered and the average cost of the procedure.

Have your doctor contact the hospital to request that you be allowed to bring your own prescriptions from home.

CHAPTER 5: *Legal*

ENLARGING THE FINE PRINT

Fortunately, or unfortunately, depending on your point of view, very little of what we do is free of some legal implication. Most laws are good but it seems some are a little more worthy of our attention than others. In Colorado, for example, it is unlawful to lend your vacuum cleaner to your next-door neighbor; in Connecticut walking backward after sunset is a no-no; if you're driving through Massachusetts with your pets, be sure the gorilla is not in the backseat; and—pass the word—bees flying over or through the streets of Kirkland, Illinois, are subject to instant arrest.

There isn't anything mysterious or intimidating about the law; most laws are common-sense ways of protecting ourselves. In this chapter we look at common legal tools and how they can help us. Let's look first at some of the items that may be in your *Life File* before tackling powers of attorney, wills, and trusts.

Your Life File

LAWSUIT CONCLUSIONS

At the end of any lawsuit the court issues a statement defining its conclusions and how the parties are obliged to conform to that decision. You will need copies in case of any later dispute. Keep them in your *Life File*.

STORED OR LOANED ITEMS

When you loan or store a valuable item, file the loan note or storage information in a bank safe deposit box or with your attorney and a photocopy in your *Life File*. Your record should include a detailed description of the item, its fair market value (with any appraisal information attached), where it is stored or to whom or what it is loaned, and the complete contact information of the person or facility that has it. In the situation of a loaned item, you should also note when you expect the item to be returned. Keep this list in your *Life File*.

INCOME TAX RETURNS

Tax returns must be kept for seven years. The reason is that the Internal Revenue Service will require your last six income tax returns if you didn't report income that they think was taxable and was more than 25% of the income shown on your current return. The

Internal Revenue Service, however, can ask for all of your tax returns. Paper copies will create a very large file. If your records are on computer disk, label each disk with the year of the return and file in your *Life File*.

LETTER OF INSTRUCTION

Most people want to be as considerate of others as possible. This is especially true at a time of stress. Your **Letter of Instruction** is one way to help your family when you no longer can. It should contain a complete list of your assets and your wishes about how your estate should be distributed and your funeral conducted.

It is a letter to family and friends about things not mentioned in your will. Most of us rarely say, even to a close friend or family member, that we want them to have an item that we cherish. So it goes unsaid. And will probably go undone. Pity.

A Letter of Instruction doesn't take the place of a will and is not legally binding so it doesn't have to be solemn and mechanical. Separate the personal details from your other wishes and write it in such a way that your unique personality shines through. ("To my little brother: I've left you my diaries—there's one page you haven't seen yet! Enjoy.") Personal letters are a long-forgotten art—but they shouldn't be. Use your Letter of Instruction to express those thoughts that, for one reason or another, were never said.

Then go on to other matters; your *Life File* already has a list of assets, and your Letter of Instruction should indicate where to locate anything else so that nothing is overlooked in settling your estate. There are probably lots of items you will want to include— each one will ease the burden on your family.

Make sure the appropriate people know where your Letter of Instruction is; keep a copy in your *Life File*. Keep it up-to-date by revising when any significant event occurs.

LIVING WILL

See *Living Will* in *Chapter 3, Medical*. Keep two or three originals in your *Life File* as well as a copy with your agent, attorney, medical provider, and medical facility.

FUNERAL AND BURIAL INSTRUCTIONS

Usually, this information is contained in your Letter of Instruction. This heading is added since "Letter of Instruction" doesn't seem to be a common term. Also see the section on *Death and Coping* later.

Powers of Attorney

Any **power of attorney** should be drafted by an attorney. Copies of all powers of attorney should be kept with your attorney. If the attorney retires or moves out of state, they are obliged to return all documents in your file. Keep photocopies in your *Life File* and give several originals to your agent. If you revoke a power of attorney, contact your agent in writing and retrieve and shred the old copy.

POWER OF ATTORNEY
FOR HEALTH CARE

See also *Power of Attorney for Health Care* in *Chapter 3, Medical*. Make a list of each person, medical service provider, or health care facility that has an original and file photocopies in your *Life File*. If you revoke a power of attorney for health care, contact your agent (in writing) and any medical facility or physician that has one to retrieve and shred the old copy.

POWER OF ATTORNEY FOR FINANCES

Have you ever read the tiny, tiny print on a credit card application? "Legal-ese" at its finest. The object is to create a revolving credit account; that's usually the first line, and all the rest are exceptions. Powers of attorney follow that tradition: there's the power of attorney and two exceptions. (The surprise is that there are only two exceptions.)

A power of attorney is a powerful, important, and useful tool. You may never have to use one, but you should be familiar with it in case you do. They're rather straightforward but, as with any legal tool, you must use it wisely.

A **power of attorney for finance** gives someone legal authority to conduct your business for you. How much authority you grant, for how long, and for what business is up to you. It is often used in the event of illness or disability or for legal transactions when you cannot be present.

The person creating a power of attorney is called the Principal. The person named on the power of attorney to make decisions or conduct your business is called the Agent or Attorney-in-Fact. Let's be very clear on this: an agent is your representative— *not* your boss. An agent can only do what they are instructed to do when they are instructed to do it. Nothing more and nothing less.

That was easy. Now let's see what the exceptions are all about.

The exceptions have to do with how long a power of attorney lasts and when it takes effect. The three options are: Durable, Nondurable, and Springing.

"Durable" means lasting or permanent. A **durable power of attorney** takes effect as soon as it is signed and lasts until it is revoked (by you) or until your death. An extremely powerful legal tool.

"Nondurable" means not lasting. A **nondurable power of attorney** also takes effect immediately and lasts until it is revoked (by you) or until you become mentally incompetent or die, *unless* you indicate specific limits on what is it for, when it will begin, and how long it will last. This type is often created for a specific business transaction. If you're on vacation and someone wants to buy that Atlantic low-tide-line property, you would want to make the sale as quickly as humanly possible. Being a very astute person, before you left on vacation you created a nondurable power of attorney and named someone to sign the real estate papers in your absence. When the papers are signed, the nondurable power of attorney ends.

"Springing" means that a power of attorney "springs" to life much like spring affects a tulip bulb. When the ground warms it signals tulip bulbs that it's time to sprout. A **springing power of attorney** works the same way: when something happens, the power of attorney becomes active.

Here's a little summary:

Power of attorney for finances: gives your agent legal authority to conduct your business.
Durable power of attorney for finances: permanent; may be revoked.

WHEN LIFE CHANGES FOREVER

Nondurable power of attorney for finances: temporary; may be revoked.

Springing power of attorney for finances: becomes effective when a certain event or events occur; may be revoked.

A **power of attorney for finance** requires an attorney, two witnesses, and must be notarized by a notary public. This is an extremely powerful tool, and you should consult an attorney before creating or signing one.

Without limiting the authority of a power of attorney for finance, the following are some examples of what an agent can do on your behalf.

* Buy or sell real estate

* Manage property

* Conduct banking transactions (make deposits or withdrawals)

* Invest money

* Make legal claims and conduct litigation

* Conduct tax and retirement matters

* Make gifts on your behalf

Signing any power of attorney is like signing a blank check—make sure the person named as your agent is trustworthy and has your best interests in mind. Never sign anything that you do not understand or do not want to sign.

Your agent is legally responsible to conduct your business honestly and in your best interests, and there are very severe penalties for misconduct. If you have signed a power of attorney, make sure the agent is following your instructions and you are getting true and complete information on any transactions. If you find there's any monkey business going on, report it to the police immediately.

You may revoke any power of attorney at any time for any reason. Inform the agent in writing that you are revoking it and ask them to return all copies. Notify your bank and other financial institutions that it has been revoked, and if it was used to buy or sell property, notify the County Clerk in the county in which the transaction took place.

An example of a power of attorney for finance can be found in the *Appendix*.

WILLS AND TRUSTS

YOUR WILL

How long would it take you to write: "Upon my death, I leave everything to my husband," have two witnesses sign their names, and a notary public notarize it? Five minutes? Ten? Fifteen, tops. That's, of course, an exaggeration, but what happens if you don't make a will? Do you really know? If not, read on (but as they say sometimes on TV, "discretion is advised"; it's not pretty).

The most obvious reason to write a will is to assure that your spouse, children, relatives, or friends receive your assets or tributes. The less-obvious reason is that if you do not (and pass away without one, or **intestate),** state laws specify how property and assets are distributed. Generally, the order in which an inheritance is passed by the state is to: spouse (one-half); children (remaining half divided among all children); or if not them, then grandchildren; parents; siblings of the deceased; and other relatives. If no heirs can be traced, all property goes to the state.

The federal government and, perhaps your state, will get their cut first through **estate ("death") taxes.** The Internal Revenue Service offers the following chart of 2007 federal tax rates for estates and trusts.

2007 Federal Estate and Trust Tax Rates	
If taxable income is:	The tax is:
Not over $2,150	15% of the taxable income
Over $2,150 but not over $5,000	$322.50 plus 25% of the excess over $2,150

2007 Federal Estate and Trust Tax Rates	
If taxable income is:	The tax is:
Over $5,000 but not over $7,650	$1,035.00 plus 28% of the excess over $5,000
Over $7,650 but not over $10,450	$1,777.00 plus 33% of the excess over $7,650
Over $10,450	$2,701.00 plus 35% of the excess over $10,450

While we all, however grudgingly, agree to pay taxes, 35% of all of your assets over $10,450 is a healthy chunk. But if you pass away without a will, that's what the government will get. How will that impact your survivors? It's a hefty price to pay for not taking the few hours to think about, write, and execute a will. You will need an attorney for this because state laws influence what can and cannot be included.

If your estate qualifies for a credit on federal estate taxes, some states impose a tax in the exact amount of the credit (boorishly called a "pick-up" tax because the state "picks up" whatever the government does not).

State inheritance tax may also be levied on the right to receive property. Beneficiaries are divided according to their relation to the deceased with different exemptions and tax rates for each; generally, the closer the relationship, the lower the tax. But taxes nevertheless.

How much of this would you like to avoid? (Hint: All of it—or as much as you can.)

I don't have an "estate," you may be thinking. You do if you're breathing. Planning and preparation aren't only for your benefit. Whether you have homes, cars, and boats or not, if you have one family heirloom, what will happen to it? That treasured vase you have carted from one place to another over a lifetime because it's been in your family for generations may get chucked onto the trash heap without your instructions. And no matter how loving family members are, if there are assets to be divided there may be hurt feelings at least or lengthy court battles at worst. If you care about these people, you need to make your wishes clear. They may not agree with your decisions, but they will honor them. Placing the burden of these decisions on others is inconsiderate.

A will is a set of instructions describing how property will be handled after death. The person making the will is called the **testator.** As long as it meets state laws, even a simple will is valid, but, of course, you should always consult an estate attorney when creating or changing a will. See the *Example of a Will Preparation Worksheet* in the *Appendix*.

A part of most wills is the appointment of an executrix. The **executrix** (female) or **executor** (male) is the person responsible for assuring that the terms of the will are carried out.

You may appoint more than one executrix, a co-executrix, and one or more successors. A successor will step in if an executrix or co-executrix cannot perform their tasks. Some attorneys and financial planners suggest naming a lawyer or bank trust officer (when a trust is established in a will) along with a family member; others advise choosing only a professional or only a family member; and yet others recommend including a provision in your will that allows your family to switch executrix, co-executrix, or successors. Since there doesn't seem to be any reliable advice on this point, make your own decisions; they're probably the best anyway.

A will is not officially recognized until a probate court has examined it, determined the circumstances under which it was signed, and declared it valid. This process is referred to as **probate**, or probating, and it is during this process that legal title to property is formally passed to the heirs. During probate, the court will either confirm the executrix named in the will or appoint another one, known as an **administrator**. It is also during the probate period that any objections to the will are reviewed by the court. If there are no protests and the executrix is acceptable to the court, the will is admitted to probate; estate assets are collected and assessed, debts are paid, and distributions made to heirs. When the administration of the estate is complete, the will becomes a public document. After probate it is very difficult to alter or upset the terms of a will and it rarely happens, but anyone's legitimate claim of fraud or coercion will be heard by the court.

Not all wills must be probated. Whether or not a will passes through probate depends on the size of the estate; in some states an estate valued at less than $600,000 is not subject to probate and "summary administrations" or "small estate" procedures are conducted. The federal threshold is $1 million. When you create a will, your attorney will advise you.

During probate, all assets and liabilities are added up and the total is what is used to calculate estate taxes. To avoid being included, placing assets in a trust is a convenience. Trust assets pass directly to trust beneficiaries and, except for Testamentary trusts, bypass probate entirely. Trusts are discussed in more detail below.

Any challenge to a will must be made through the court. The two most common reasons for contesting a will are assertions that the deceased's thinking was too muddled to draft a legally binding will, and that the deceased was influenced by a third party. During the time a dispute or challenge is reviewed by the court, money in the form of legal fees is being withdrawn from the estate, leaving less for beneficiaries and heirs.

Some people recommend videotaping the will signing or obtaining medical and psychological evaluations to prove that the deceased was lucid. With videotaping, the reasons for how and why the estate is divided can be clearly explained but it can backfire if the person looks confused or tired—which can happen when people are sick, elderly, or just camera-shy. Medical or psychological evaluations have a life span; if they were obtained ten years before the will entered probate they have no value.

A common thread in estate disputes is lack of communication. Discuss your plans with your heirs but keep them out of the actual estate-planning process to prevent later claims of undue influence. Think about placing assets in a trust or using a "no contest" clause. Adding a no-contest clause reduces the chances of a legal challenge; it's a paragraph that states that anyone who contests the will shall only be entitled to inherit $1.00 or some minor token.

The hardest part of passing on your wealth, whether it's $100 or $100 million, isn't trying to decipher tax codes or trust laws. It's the emotional stuff—figuring out how to divide your assets so that family members aren't hurt or disappointed. If you have a harmonious family, the number one thing you want to do is to keep it that way. It is probably the most overlooked facet of inheritance planning not only by professionals but family members. Family members are reluctant to talk about dying and what happens to the people and property left behind. Professionals have no idea about your family dynamics. It's up to you.

Where to start? Discussing your plans in advance can yield big benefits: the chance to gauge people's feelings and reactions. Even if you don't change your plans, ask each person separately what they expect or want. Of course, talking about your plans won't guarantee that anyone will agree with them, but these are your decisions. Make the best ones you can and don't look back.

Providing for the less able. When appropriate, family estate plans should allow for current or potential disabilities; unknown needs at unknown times or a "broad clause" that provides for beneficiaries with emotional or physical issues, or even for heirs who are unprepared to deal with an inheritance for reasons other than disabilities. Money or income-generating assets can be held in trust and used for their benefit and not distributed outright. The object is to protect such beneficiaries from frivolously spending or mishandling their inheritance.

Families with emotionally, physically, or developmentally challenged children or adults should plan early and wisely. Making arrangements for their care is fraught with complications and it takes special expertise to navigate complex trust agreements, government benefit programs, and medical insurance. Get expert professional advice as soon as possible.

For children or adults who will never lead a fully independent life, look into setting up a special needs trust.

The word "trust" has come up many times so far. Let's see what they are in the next section.

TRUSTS

Trusts are very flexible legal tools that come in all shapes and sizes: custodial trusts for property and assets, life insurance trusts in which the trust is the beneficiary of a life insurance policy, trusts for minors and dependents, special needs trusts, charitable trusts, maintenance trusts for interment sites, pet care trusts, and whatever (within the law) you want to accomplish.

A trust is like your own private corporation; let's call it Julie's Wonderful Trust. You set it up to do what you want, hire people to run it, put money in (or take it out), have control over everything in it until you let someone else (the trustee) take over, distribute (or not) earnings, and end it whenever you like or let it roll on as long as it can.

A trust is a legal arrangement created for the ownership and management of real property or other assets by someone other than its current owner. It is managed by one or more trustees for the benefit of one or more beneficiaries. As well as real estate and cash, investments (such as mutual funds, stocks, bonds, certificates of deposit, annuities, and other income-producing assets) may be transferred to a trust.

Some assets shouldn't be placed in a trust, of course: your personal checking/savings account, property you intend to sell, vehicles, individual retirement plans, profit-sharing plans, employer stock option plans, and the income and/or principal from another trust.

As usual, let's get the definitions out of the way first.

Fiduciary responsibility   When someone is entrusted with the management of assets or with the power to act on someone's behalf, they have a duty to perform these tasks in the best interests of that person (trust or estate). For example, an executrix or executor of an estate must make decisions that are in the best interests of the estate; a trustee must make decisions that are in the best interests of the trust. There are very stiff legal penalties if a person does not perform their duties honestly and responsibly.

Grantor   The one establishing the trust and funding it (putting in the money or assets).

Trustee   The person or entity (a bank for example) that runs the trust. More than one person or entity may be appointed as trustees or co-trustees. They must have a very high standard of integrity to meet their fiduciary responsibility to manage the property or money and see that it is used only for the stated purpose and intent of the trust.

Successor trustee   When a trustee is appointed

to manage a trust, often a successor trustee is also appointed in case the trustee is unable to perform their functions.

Living or **Revocable trust** A living or revocable trust is established during the grantor's life. Its terms can be changed or it may be revoked at any time for any reason. During the term of a living trust, the original owner of the property has control over the property unless and until they specify otherwise.

Testamentary trust A trust established in a will. A testamentary trust is not subject to change and is not revocable. Testamentary trusts must be probated, and assets cannot be transferred out of the trust until probate is complete.

Irrevocable trust Since most irrevocable trusts are established by a will, the grantor is no longer able to revoke it or change its terms. Should you decide to create an irrevocable trust during your lifetime, you can never change its terms, revoke it, or withdraw assets. An irrevocable trust is an independent entity under the law.

Unfunded trust An unfunded trust may just be the paperwork to create a trust and may be considered a viable trust for some time after the paperwork is created even though it doesn't have anything in it; it is designated to receive assets in the future. However, in some states, a nominal funding (say, $100) is required to legally establish a trust.

Funded trust   To function, a trust must have

funds or assets formally transferred into it. For our example, to be included in Julie's Wonderful Trust, the name of the owner on the deed of a condo must be changed to "Julie's Wonderful Trust." As soon as that is done, the property becomes a part of the trust and all proceeds from the property are deposited into the trust account.

Trust assets are owned by the trust. Examples of trust property may be homes, rental property, mutual funds, art, collectibles, and other tangible (real) assets. When assets are included in a trust, the name of the owner on the title of the asset must be changed to the name of the trust. Any income from the asset goes to the trust. Even in community property states, any asset transferred to a trust is separate. In community property states, property transferred to a trust should be clearly identified as having been community property and the trust documents must identify it as property that will revert to its community-property status if the trust is revoked.

The primary reasons to create a trust are its tax implications and to avoid lengthy probate. A trust may reduce or eliminate federal estate taxes for both spouse's estates, while at the same time preserving trust assets for the benefit of its current owner. Trusts can also provide financial support for others while the grantor retains control of the income-generating asset(s). A trust is particularly useful for parents in second marriages.

A trust is an ongoing reminder of your generosity. To assure that it does not become a burden to its beneficiaries, consult a trust attorney and a tax accountant to deal with the legal, tax, accounting, investment, and administrative details.

The terms of a trust are not made public. Trusts ensure that the property or assets will be responsibly managed should the grantor become incapacitated or incapable of managing their affairs. Trusts may provide for regular asset distribution as designated by the grantor. A living trust has the ability to cross state lines; if you have property in another state held in a living trust, probating a will in each state will not be necessary. A living trust preserves assets, or income-generating property, for the current and future benefit of a surviving spouse and/or beneficiaries.

When planning for or anticipating disability, whether long- or short-term, the living trust is a useful tool. Income from assets under trustee management can be made available at any time. When spouses serve as co-trustees, the terms of the trust may allow either to act independently; that is, in a situation when one spouse becomes unable because of illness or disability, the other can manage the trust. When the illness or disability is resolved, that spouse can resume their role of trustee.

A living trust can avoid months, if not years, of legal proceedings and ongoing court supervision. A will and testamentary trust, by definition, are not effective during one's lifetime so cannot offer these benefits.

Creating a Trust. The trust officer of your local bank or a trust attorney can set up a trust. This is not something you want to do on your own; trusts are established to achieve specific goals and there are legal and tax considerations.

All financial institutions require authorization in the form of the trust documents before they will execute the transaction instructions of a trustee.

Who's in charge? As with all legal instruments involving delegating authority and responsibility to others, think carefully before appointing trustees and selecting beneficiaries. You are creating a legacy from which future generations will benefit; with a living trust you are in charge; with a testamentary trust created in a will you have defined the terms— how it works out you can only hope.

Choosing a Trustee. First, find the best person for the job. You can structure the trust with as many guides, dictates, limits, exceptions, inclusions, and provisions as you want, but if the trustee doesn't understand them or is unwilling or unable to fulfill their goals, roll up the papers and use them to fire up the BBQ.

Basically, there are two considerations: management

and application. The distinction between making money and managing it is clear to all of us. The trustee must be able to reasonably and, hopefully, profitably manage the assets (management). They must also be able to apply the income in the manner you have set forth to create the greatest benefit (application). Establishing spouses as co-trustees is simple and effective. Most trusts are straightforward and consist largely of family real estate and funds. Unless otherwise agreed, professional trustees reasonably require a minimum payscale that is often a percentage of the value of the trust or its income. Non-professional trustees should agree on compensation beforehand. Whatever you decide, it should be clearly stated in the terms of the trust.

BENEFITS OF A TRUST

Beside avoiding certain taxes, the common reason for creating a living trust is to help or support those either too young or unable to maintain an adequate or desirable quality of life. The nature of a trust is to generate income and principal and distribute it.

Except for charitable trusts that may continue indefinitely, a grantor must decide the trust's time limit. The limit can be quite broad and can span three generations; the grantor's lifetime, grantor's first-tier beneficiaries (children), and second-tier beneficiaries (grandchildren). The grantor must also decide on the disposition of any funds remaining at the end of the trust's life.

Special Needs Trusts. For children or adults who will be unable to lead fully independent lives, look into special needs trusts. Often funded by annuities or life insurance, this type of trust is a security shield; it protects the child/adult from losing state and federal social services that provide food, shelter, and clothing (under Social Security and Medicare) even as it maintains their eligibility for Medicaid. Trust money can be used for supplementary goods and services over and above other benefits and other family members can also donate to them.

Final caveat: Beware of prepackaged living trust scams that promise to solve all your tax, financial, and probate problems. They won't.

DEATH AND COPING

No matter how well we think we are prepared for or equipped to handle the death of a spouse, child, or loved one, we may be overwhelmed by its devastation. After a long illness, we say, "It's a blessing," and think we will move on. And, indeed, we will. But sometimes the event is so shocking and unexpected that we find ourselves in a state bordering on inertia. In the next hours and days we will be confronted with decisions that will impact the rest of our lives. Relying on the advice of family and friends, people make important decisions with little or no knowledge of what is involved or the consequences of the actions that they do, or do not, take.

But this doesn't have to be the case.

When a partner dies there are financial and personal issues that must be dealt with immediately. Most of us know very little about funerals, how they are handled, what documents are needed, how to pay for them, and have only a vague idea of the deceased's wishes. But somehow it will magically happen and your spouse's funeral will be as you expect in every detail. We are comforted by the knowledge that our estate—homes, cars, and businesses—will sustain us and that we will manage our new lives in some kind of peace and order.

It's a mesmerizing scenario but the truth is very different, although it's not as frightening as you may think. There's lots of help available. Don't push the panic button yet; let's walk through some of the steps first.

Someone you love has died. You are faced with the difficult and slow, one-day-at-a-time work (and it is work) of acknowledging their absence and coping with your loss. You may be overwhelmed with loneliness, anxiety, and depression, thoughts of "what might have been," and wrenching memories of lost hopes and unfulfilled dreams. How can you survive the pain and sadness when you feel so empty and abandoned? There are no magical formulas to remove your suffering. The best solution to grief is to grieve.

Pace yourself. Try to reduce the pressure by accepting help from others; you have enough on your plate without adding to it. Grief is exhausting. You need to replenish yourself to do the things that must be done at the least-stressful pace. Respect what your body and mind are telling you. Nurture yourself; rest, eat balanced meals, and lighten your schedule. Caring for yourself doesn't mean wallowing in self-pity; it means surviving. You are facing a new and unfamiliar world. You need to adjust, develop, and get used to new routines, learn to handle new responsibilities, and how to interact with people in new ways. Discovering what this new world is all about and learning how to cope with it is part of mourning. It's a lot to accomplish.

Before any arrangements can be made, a **Coroner** or **Medical Examiner** will be notified, depending on the circumstances of the death. For most deaths their services will not be required. Each state has its own laws, but they will generally become involved if the deceased was unattended at the time of death, when a doctor is unable to determine the cause of death, if the death was a homicide or suicide or the result of an accident, or the death occurred in a hospital under certain circumstances. In these situations, the authorities may order an **autopsy** which is a clinical procedure to determine the person's health during life and how they died. Unless required by law, an autopsy requires your permission. You may deny permission or request that it be performed by a doctor you name. Medical industry practice is not to charge for an autopsy and it may be performed at a hospital, funeral home, or other appropriate location.

After a death, one of the most difficult issues is what to do with personal items. It's a painful process but one that can ease your grief; it brings memories and connects you with forgotten feelings. But sometimes too many reminders can overwhelm us. The only standards are *yours;* do exactly as you wish and take your own sweet time about it, whether it's hours, days, weeks, years, or never. Donating clothes, for example, doesn't mean "getting rid" of them; it allows someone else to enjoy them.

THE FUNERAL

Long before recorded history, funeral rites memorialized the lives of our ancestors. Evidence of ritual burials have been found in every culture and corner of the earth. In our society, however, our attitude toward death is a paradox; mostly we ignore its inevitability, yet it represents a huge emotional and economic investment. In an industry estimated at $20 billion a year, 70% of all funeral arrangements are made by women. Funeral expenses represent one of the top five largest investments most people make in their lifetime.

Before going any further, let's chat about asking questions and shopping. Shopping is good. Asking questions is good. Saving money is better than both. And all three are a "hat trick" when you must purchase items that you probably know little about; not many people buy caskets, for example, ahead of time, and a casket can represent as much as a third of the total cost of a funeral.

The first question that jumps to mind is: "Isn't shopping in this situation in poor taste?" and the answer is: "That's the wrong question." No question is wrong (unless, of course, if it's about your age), but taste and judgment are two different things. Someone else's ideas about what you need or want are not the road you want to travel right now. This is definitely a time for informed decision making and not a time to impoverish yourself for the future. The point is, whether you have a large or small budget, it is pointless to overspend. And chances are very good that you will overspend for a funeral if you don't know what you want and need.

It will certainly ease the burden on family and friends if your plans are complete before the need arises (see *Pre-Planning* below) and you have written a Letter of Instruction (above).

Funeral practices are influenced by religious and cultural traditions, the circumstances of the death, costs, and personal preferences. These factors determine if a funeral will be elaborate or simple, public or private, religious or secular, and where and how it will be held. They also influence if the body will be present, if there will be viewing or visiting hours, if the casket will be open or closed, or if remains will be buried or cremated. Don't worry, there's plenty of help and, of course, information in the *Appendix*.

For any funeral there are two separate costs: funeral services and goods, and cemetery (or interment) goods and services. You cannot purchase interment goods and services from a funeral service provider, nor funeral products and services from a cemetery owner. (See the checklist in the *Appendix*.)

Among the many choices available, the industry recognizes three basic types of services.

Traditional or full-service funeral. Considered the most expensive, it may include a casket, viewing hours, a formal funeral service (at the funeral parlor and/or religious site and/or burial site), use of a hearse and other vehicles, and/or cremation. In addition to the funeral home's basic service fees, there may be other costs such as for embalming, dressing, cash-advance items, and extras (flowers, **obituary** notices, acknowledgment cards, or limousines) that can add thousands of dollars; today many funerals run well over $6,000.

Direct burial. In this service the remains are buried shortly after death, usually in a simple container without embalming. (Embalming is a method of preservation and is not a required part of the funeral process in any state. The cost of embalming varies and often begins around $500. If direct burial is planned, there is no need for embalming.) No viewing hours are held and a memorial service may be held at the interment location, religious site, or funeral home. Costs may include a funeral home's basic service fee, transportation, and casket or burial container costs.

Direct Cremation. Cremation occurs shortly after death without embalming. (If direct cremation is planned, there is no need for embalming and it is not required by any state law.) After the cremation process, remains are placed in an urn or other container. No viewing hours are scheduled and a memorial service may be held with or without the remains present at the inurnment or interment location, religious site, or funeral home. Costs may include the funeral home's basic fee, transportation, a crematory fee, and the cost of an urn or other container, unless you provide one (see *Urns* below). Funeral providers that offer cremation must also offer an alternative container (in place of a casket) for the cremation process (see *Casket/ Coffin* below).

Your choices of goods and services are personal decisions that should be reviewed with the funeral director. Bring a friend or family member when visiting the funeral director for emotional support and to help review your options. All funeral directors are required to show or give you a price list of all their services and products. When visiting a funeral director, consider the following:

* The funeral home must provide the prices for each of their goods and services as well as a price list for caskets and cremation items (and they can sometimes offer price information on vaults and grave liners).

* If you plan to take care of certain services (placing death notices in the newspaper or religious services) and these charges are included in the basic fee, ask that they be removed.

* Embalming is sometimes included when it is not needed. Ask the funeral director if it is necessary (and see below).

* Many preparation services may be included in the basic fee. Ask exactly what services are included and insist that a charge be removed if you do not want the service or product or it is not needed for the type of service planned. For example, cosmetology and dressing would not be appropriate for a closed-casket service, direct burial, or direct cremation.

CHOOSING A FUNERAL HOME

Often the selection of a funeral service provider is based on location, religion, past service, or a friend's recommendation. Limiting your search to one facility may risk paying more than necessary or restricting your choices of goods and services. Comparing goods and services is prudent and not difficult if you have the time.

The funeral director is required to show you, or give you, a list of all of their products and services, called a **General Price List.** You may find it less stressful to telephone, but either way you need to know the costs of all services and merchandise.

The General Price List may be several pages long. Don't be misled; it's a sales gimmick. This is big business and they want you to buy, buy, buy. Buy only what you need. By and large we are middle-of-the-roaders and when offered a selection of several items will select one of the first three. Every funeral director and salesperson in the world knows this about you. If you're shown three items that cost $1,000, $1,500, and $2,000, there is an excellent chance you'll select the $1,500 item. That's why the most expensive items in any showroom are the first ones you see.

At its most basic, funeral services include:

* Funeral planning

* Securing necessary permits
* Copies of death certificates (see *Death Certificates* below)
* Sheltering remains
* Coordinating arrangements with interment and/or religious sites
* Preparing notices

Other goods and services may include:

* Transportation (from place of death to funeral home to interment site)
* Embalming and cosmetology (embalming may or may not be required; cosmetology includes hair care, make-up, and dressing)
* Use of the funeral home for viewing, ceremony, or memorial service. These may be separate charges. Be sure to clarify the price for viewing and/or visiting hours. Is the price quoted for all sessions or just one?
* Use of equipment and staff at graveside (set up/use of tents and chairs)
* Use of a hearse or limousine(s)
* Casket and drapery

What the Funeral Director Needs:

* The deceased's birth certificate and Social Security number

* Any written request for services

* Payment for cash-advance items

* Insurance policy(ies)

* Veteran's service number or record

What You Need:

Death certificates. The funeral director will provide death certificates. Get several copies (ten) for use at financial institutions, the Social Security Administration, Veterans Administration, and insurance companies. Traditionally, part of the funeral director's service is to submit copies to the interment facility and appropriate state and government agencies.

Newspaper obituary. A death notice must appear in a local paper at least once. It may also be appropriate for publication in newspapers elsewhere (for example, if you recently moved, neighbors at your former address may want to know). Most newspapers have their own guidelines for what to include.

Out-of-town guests. Being able to provide the names of local hotels will be helpful to guests traveling from a distance. Post a list with phone numbers and directions near your phone or perhaps a friend or relative would serve as a travel resource.

After services. Often friends and relatives gather at the home of the bereaved or a relative or at a commercial location after services. If you are hosting such a gathering, serve light refreshments, and if many visitors are expected, it may be appropriate to hire caterers. Or you may prefer to have a luncheon or similar function elsewhere; contact the venue to order the menu.

Cards. Most funeral homes have a selection of cards (at a cost) to acknowledge guests, participants, or contributions (flowers or donations). They also provide a guest book (at a cost). It is from the guest book that you can get the names, and sometimes addresses for guests, for sending cards. Acknowledgement cards should be sent within one month.

Clergy/Religious site. The funeral director's professional service fees may, or may not, include scheduling religious services. The director can coordinate services with a religious establishment, but costs for religious services are separate. The funeral director can give you details and contact information. Services may be held at the funeral home, a religious site, both, or elsewhere, it's up to you.

Pallbearers. Pallbearers accompany the casket from the funeral home to interment location. Being a **pallbearer** is an honor, not a right. You make the decisions on who they will be or if pallbearers will be used. Call prospective pallbearers as soon as possible and give a list of their names and telephone numbers to the funeral director.

Eulogy. A **eulogy** is usually a sensitive, heartfelt tribute. And then there are others...people who simply talk too much, bring up inappropriate topics, or who are more into theater than remembrance. And, worst of all, they can't be stopped once they get started, like a really bad karaoke performance. To avoid this situation, have the person giving the eulogy write it out for you and keep it short (under ten minutes). Only share upbeat recollections; making people cry at a funeral is just plain mean. Have the speaker focus on the deceased; ask them not to talk exclusively about their relationship with the deceased and to mention other friends or relatives. Give a copy of the remarks to a stand-in in case they don't feel up to it at the last minute; it happens. And finally, sometimes the most eloquent eulogy is a moment of silence.

Transportation. If funeral home limousines will be used, the director will need a list of who is to be transported in each car. Usually, the closer a person is related by blood to the deceased, the closer they are to the hearse. But, here again, you make the decisions.

Flowers. Flowers are a personal preference. Some people request (in the newspaper obituary) that instead of flowers, a donation be made to a charity or other worthy cause.

For military, police, and fire there are strict funeral protocols and a representative of the group will explain them to you, but the decisions, as always, are yours.

FUNERARY MERCHANDISE

Funeral service providers are businesses. Their profits depend on sales, and caskets are the largest cost items they sell. No one would deny a business a reasonable profit, but you must think about how much you can afford to spend. Social Security provides a one-time benefit of $255 and insurance will help. If you are purchasing a valuable casket and many extras, costs can get out of control in short order. How will this expense impact your future?

The usual items purchased from funeral homes are the use of their facility, transportation, caskets, and urns. (Vaults and grave liners may—but not always—be purchased from either a cemetery or funeral home. Crypts, niches, and cemetery plots are purchased from a cemetery, columbarium, or mausoleum, discussed below.) Because these goods and services are offered doesn't mean that purchasing them from the funeral service provider is your only option; it is not. And it does not mean that you need all services and products; you do not. The final decisions are yours.

Casket/Coffin. A **casket** or coffin is a container or chest for burying remains and a sanitary and acceptable means of transport from one location to another. Typically constructed of metal, fiberboard, fiberglass, plastic, mahogany, or clad in bronze, or copper, they vary widely in style and price. Caskets can represent over 30% of all funeral charges. You do not have to purchase a casket from the funeral home and should clearly understand when you need one. When cremation is used, very carefully consider the choice of casket. In most states, funeral homes are required to offer an alternate, inexpensive container for the cremation process. If viewing will be part of the funeral, consider some of the options below.

As a separate purchase (that is, not from the funeral home), remember that caskets must meet cemetery standards and must take the size of the body into account. Shop wisely; retail casket sellers are not bound by the same laws or regulations that govern funeral establishments or interment locations.

No matter where you purchase it, no casket, regardless of its quality or cost, will preserve a body forever. Terms such as "gasketed," "protective," or "sealer" mean that a rubber gasket or some other device or manufacturing process has been added to delay the penetration of groundwater or to prevent rust. Claims that these features help preserve the remains indefinitely are simply hype; they do not, they just add cost. Some caskets come with a warranty for longevity or workmanship. If this is an extra cost, ask yourself: how would you prove that its longevity was unsatisfactory?

Another option is renting. When a funeral includes viewing hours, the funeral parlor may have an acceptable casket that may be rented. You will need to purchase a container for burial (or cremation), but then you can select a model that meets your budget.

If you select an inexpensive or rental model, consider draping it; if the deceased is a veteran, the flag is appropriate; a blanket of flowers can be used; and funeral parlors have a cloth, or drape, for the purpose.

Don't think of these options as compromises; think of how these costs will affect you later. Will it take a substantial amount of your income over the next three years to pay for the funeral? Be realistic.

Embalming. **Embalming** is a temporary preservation technique employed for open-casket viewing, when the body will be transported interstate, or if burial will take place more than twenty-four hours after death. There is a fee for embalming; all funeral homes must have permission for this process and it is not a required part of any funeral. It is a practical necessity and required if:

* there will be public or private viewing (open casket);

* to enhance the deceased's appearance;

* the body will be transported by air or rail;

* because of the length of time between time of death and burial;

* the funeral home shelters the remains for more than twenty-four hours; and

* it does not conflict with religious beliefs, legal requirements, or medical examination.

Throughout history, charlatans have claimed that embalming oils, herbs, and special body preparations will preserve remains indefinitely. To date, no such preparations have been invented (even ancient Egyptians were not completely able to preserve their dead). Don't fall for it.

Cremation. Cremation is an irreversible process that eliminates determining the exact cause of death. The process exposes the remains to extreme heat and flame. For this reason, many states require that a Coroner or Medical Examiner authorize each cremation, and some states have specific minimum time limits before a cremation can take place. The funeral director will know the state law.

If cremation is chosen, you or the person responsible for the deceased must authorize it with a separate contract. The contract includes the location, time, disposition of remains (ashes) after the process, and an agreement for payment.

The following methods for the disposition of cremated remains may be available in your area:

* placement in a columbarium or mausoleum (see below);

* burial in a cemetery plot;

* retention by spouse, relative, or friend;

* storage at a house of worship or religious site; or

* scattering at some location; a cemetery scattering garden, or at sea.

All local laws must be observed; the funeral director will know them.

Urns. An urn is a repository for cremated remains. It may be purchased from the funeral home, somewhere else, or you can provide one. Discuss these options before the cremation process, as the size of the urn is important.

INTERMENT

Interment in a grave is the most common type of burial. Cemeteries are divided into two broad categories: traditional cemeteries and memorial parks (or gardens). A traditional cemetery has upright stone monuments or ground-level plaques and may have private mausoleums (see below) for above-ground entombment. Memorial parks and gardens do not accept upright tombstones but prefer to maintain the landscape and will install only markers that are flat and set at ground level.

There are public and private cemeteries, commercial cemeteries, and national cemeteries for veterans. Most cemeteries are zoned for type (that is, for traditional upright monuments or garden/park-like settings, and may also have a mausoleum and/or columbarium). Zones within these areas may be subdivided by cost.

When purchasing space in a cemetery consider:

* Location

* Cost

* Size of space

* Religious preferences

* Monument/marker, floral, and access (visiting hours) restrictions

* Regulations on burial vaults or grave liners.

Cemetery property is sold in units (or "plots") large enough for a single grave and, naturally, you may buy as many as you want. The most common purchase is a double lot for two graves side by side.

Due to space constraints, cemeteries close to metropolitan areas are more expensive than in urban areas. Some cemeteries have both indoor and outdoor or private mausoleums (see below).

Ask about floral or access restrictions. Some cemeteries are quite strict about what floral tokens may be left at a grave site. Access refers to visiting days and times.

MAUSOLEUM

A **mausoleum** is a building designed for above-ground entombment. It serves the same purpose as a cemetery plot, except it is above ground. Shared costs make "community" mausoleums more affordable than private ones. Within the structure, spaces, called "**crypts**" for caskets and "**niches**" for urns, may accommodate a single casket or urn or as many as twelve.

Following casket **entombment** (a term that distinguishes it from in-ground burial), the crypt is sealed with a granite or marble front. The front may be engraved or a plaque may be attached to it to identify the deceased. Niches (smaller than crypt spaces) for urns are also available and sealed in the same manner.

Selecting a mausoleum eliminates the need for burial vaults, grave liners, and monuments but may be more expensive than a cemetery. When selecting this type of facility, the level at which the remains will be located is important; these structures are a couple of stories high so ground-floor, eye-level placement is the most expensive.

Costs include crypt or niche purchase, opening and closing fees, engraving or plaque, endowment care, and other services. (Endowment care is a fund earmarked for facility maintenance, see below.) Be sure you completely understand all charges.

COLUMBARIUM

A **columbarium** is often located within a mausoleum (or chapel within a mausoleum) but may be free-standing either indoors or outdoors. **Inurnment** in a columbarium is restricted to urns.

Selecting a columbarium eliminates the need for burial vaults, grave liners, and monuments but does not eliminate the charges for purchase, opening and closing, engraving or plaque, and endowment care. When selecting this type of facility, be aware of the level at which the remains will be located; these structures are a couple of stories high, so ground-floor, eye-level is the most expensive. Be sure you completely understand all charges.

INTERMENT SERVICES

Opening/Closing Graves, Crypts, or *Niches.* Fees for these services may include fifty or more separate services, most of which you don't have to worry about, as they involve state and local permits that are handled by the funeral director or mausoleum or columbarium owner. Among other things, they typically include: administration and permanent recordkeeping, determining ownership, obtaining permission, and maintaining registration and other legal files; locating the site, surveying its boundaries; and maintenance of the site before, during, and after services. Of course, these services are more costly on weekends.

Double Depth. Many cemeteries allow two caskets in a single plot. The first is placed at a much deeper depth and the second is placed above at the standard depth. Check with the site manager or funeral director, as double-depth interment is generally restricted and not common.

Disinterment. **Disinterment** is the removal of a casket from a grave. Laws vary, but disinterment may be ordered by public officials without the consent of the owner or next of kin, as part of a police investigation. To arrange for disinterment to relocate remains contact the site owner.

Endowment Care. A portion of the grave, crypt, or niche purchase cost is contributed to an **endowment**

care fund or trust for facility maintenance and grounds upkeep or may be a separate cost. The minimum contribution is established by law and monitored by the state. Costs vary widely, and some cemeteries are permitted to collect more than the minimum amount to build the endowment fund when only the interest earned on the fund is used for site care, maintenance, and embellishment.

Perpetual Care. **Perpetual care** is whatever the cemetery, mausoleum, or columbarium owner says it is. As an optional service it is not regulated by law. If it is included in the purchase price, be careful that you understand what it includes and exactly how much it costs.

INTERMENT MERCHANDISE

Most cemeteries require outer burial chambers (called vaults) or grave liners to avoid ground settling.

Vaults and *Grave Liners.* A burial **vault**, sometimes referred to as an "outer burial container," is a container that surrounds the casket in concrete or other material for in-ground protection and to avoid ground settling. It is more substantial (and expensive) than a **grave liner** that is an oblong concrete or steel slab that rests above the casket. The purpose of both is to prevent ground settling, and most cemeteries require the use of one or the other. Vaults are not intended to prevent decomposition and will not keep water, dirt, or other debris from penetrating the casket indefinitely. Since there is a considerable difference in the price of a vault and that of a grave liner, ask about the cemetery's policy (they probably accept both).

Monuments and *markers*. All cemeteries and memorial parks or gardens have strict policies on the type, size, and construction of **markers** or **monuments**. The rule of thumb is that cemeteries allow upright monuments and memorial parks and gardens do not. Some facilities have zones for different types of markers/monuments.

Monuments and markers are usually purchased from third parties (that is, not from the cemetery) but must meet cemetery standards. If a "stone" is purchased from a retailer, cemeteries cannot charge a setting fee if the retailer installs it. Other charges, for permits or foundations, will be charged by the cemetery no matter where you get the stone. Ask about the cemetery's rules, costs, and policies, and the funeral director may be able to help you with this information.

Some cemeteries or third parties accept prepayment for markers, monuments, grave liners, and/or vaults and store them until needed. The purchase contract should contain specific information on manufacturer, model, inscriptions, a description of materials used, and the exact location of storage. The funeral director or cemetery manager will have details.

INTERMENT COSTS

The first and major cost item is for the grave plot, crypt, or niche, and costs vary considerably across the country. For cemeteries in densely populated areas (large cities), space is limited and prices are high; urban centers are more expensive than rural areas. Within each setting, location (or zone) will influence cost. For example, near a feature, such as a sculpture, waterfall, or other landscape amenity, may be more expensive than elsewhere. The interment site manager will have all the information you need and the funeral director may also be helpful.

FUNERAL PREPLANNING AND PREARRANGEMENT

Preplanning and prearrangements allow time for comparison shopping; to consider options and make changes as you learn more; and family discussion. During preplanning don't sign anything before you're ready. If you change your mind after you sign a contract, there may be a charge for changing the plan and some changes may be excluded. Following are some other issues you might wish to consider.

* Know your rights. You must receive a general price list from the funeral director or, at least, review their list. Know which products and services are required by law and which are optional.

* Avoid emotional overspending. Having the fanciest casket or the most elaborate ceremony could mean financial hardship later. Take a relative or friend when visiting funeral homes or cemeteries to discuss these issues.

* Resist pressure to buy goods, services, or packages of goods and services that contain items you do not want or need. Get everything in writing and don't sign anything you have not read or do not understand.

* Avoid any and all non-declinable fees. Non-declinable fees are for items that you must purchase. For example, if embalming is a non-declinable fee and you have chosen direct burial or direct cremation, you will be paying for a service you do not need and that probably will not be performed.

* Make provisions for change. Over time, prices will rise, businesses will close or change ownership, you may move away, or just change your mind. If the funeral home you are working with is a part of a large chain, are you able to relocate the plan to a different area? If you have prepaid for services and ownership of the facility changes, what are your rights, who will safeguard them, and how will you be notified? Funeral homes and licensed cemeteries are obligated to present a copy of

any signed pre-need agreements to the person making arrangements. If a local service provider has closed and its records have been removed to a larger corporation or merely archived, they may be unavailable. Keep a copy of any plans in your *Life File*, with your attorney, and be sure that family and friends know about them.

* Pre-Paid or Pre-Need Payment Options. Most prudent financial planners discourage the use of prepayment plans. State laws differ (or don't exist) and offer little or no protection. There are many other options available. But if you decide to prepay funeral and/cemetery services, there are probably as many plans as there are service providers.

* Pre-Need Trusts can be created with funeral establishments or interment facilities. You decide on the goods and services you want, sign a contract that fully describes each item, and pay a set amount into a trust. (Always consult an attorney when signing any contract and they should keep your original in their file; keep a photocopy in your *Life File*.)

Funeral homes are not insurance companies and are not governed by the same laws as financial or insurance institutes. When buying pre-need plans, the following are some questions you might ask.

* Who holds the funds?

* How is the fund administered?

* What management and/or overhead fees are charged?

* What are the revocation/cancellation fees?

* Does it cost to make changes in arrangements; what are they?

Put your wishes for how you want your funeral conducted in writing (see *Letter of Instruction* above). Give copies to family members and your attorney and keep a copy in your **Life File**. Do not put your only copy in a safe-deposit box or include your wishes in a will, as both of these won't be opened or read until after the funeral. If you have prepaid for any arrangements, advise family, friends, and your attorney.

VETERANS FUNERAL BENEFITS

Any honorably or generally discharged veteran is entitled to burial in one of the national cemeteries or state-operated veterans cemeteries. Contact the state cemetery or state Veterans Affairs (VA) office for more information (www.cem.va.gov). The following information is excerpted from that site.

Government benefits include a gravesite in any of our national cemeteries with available space, the opening and closing of the grave, perpetual care, a Government headstone or marker, a burial flag to drape the casket or accompany the urn, a grave liner, and a Presidential Memorial Certificate at no cost.

Markers: Upon request, the VA will furnish at no charge to the applicant, a government headstone or marker for the grave of any deceased eligible veteran in any cemetery around the world. For all deaths occurring before September 11, 2001, the VA may provide a headstone or marker only for graves that are not marked with a private headstone. Flat markers in granite, marble, and bronze and upright headstones in granite and marble are available. Niche markers are also available to mark columbaria. Spouses and dependents buried in a private cemetery are not eligible for a government-provided headstone or marker.

To apply for a U.S. flag, complete VA Form 21–2008, Application for United States Flag for Burial Purposes. You may get a flag at any VA regional office or U.S. Post Office. The funeral director will help you or call your VA regional office at 1–800–827–1000.

A Presidential Memorial Certificate is an engraved paper certificate, signed by the current President, to honor the memory of honorably discharged deceased veterans. Eligible recipients include the deceased veteran's next of kin and loved ones. More than one certificate may be provided. Apply in person at any VA regional office or by U.S. mail only. Requests cannot be sent via email. There is no form to complete but be sure to enclose a death certificate and a copy (not the original) of the veteran's discharge, to:

Presidential Memorial Certificates (41A1C)
Department of Veterans Affairs
5109 Russell Road
Quantico, VA 22134–3903

Burial Allowances are available under some circumstances.

Eligible service-related death benefit: VA will pay up to $2,000 toward burial expenses for deaths on or after September 11, 2001, and $1,500 for deaths prior to September 10, 2001. If the veteran is buried in a VA national cemetery, some or all of the cost of transporting the deceased may be reimbursed.

Eligible nonservice-related death benefit: VA will pay up to $300 toward burial and funeral expenses: for deaths on or after December 1, 2001, a $300 plot-interment allowance or $150 for deaths prior to December 1, 2001. If the death happened while the veteran was in a VA hospital or under VA contracted nursing home care, some or all of the costs for transporting the deceased's remains may be reimbursed.

Apply for burial benefits by filling out VA Form 21–530, Application for Burial Benefits. Attach a copy of proof of the veteran's military service (DD 214), a death certificate and copies of funeral and burial bills you have paid.

Female veterans receive exactly the same benefits as male veterans. Eligibility for interment in a national cemetery is extended to some civilians who have provided military-related service and some public health service personnel.

Other Issues. When death occurs at a place other than where interment will take place (in a different town, state, or country), contact the funeral provider in your hometown. They can make arrangements for transportation and advise you of its manner and cost. (If you contact a funeral director at the place of death you risk being charged twice: for their services, which may be at their highest rates, as well as for the services provided by your local director.) If a common carrier (commercial airline or railroad) is involved, the body must be embalmed prior to shipping; or, if this is not possible, an airtight container is required. You may also arrange (through your local funeral service provider) for cremation at the place of death and shipment of the cremated remains.

When death occurs in a foreign country, the resident United States Consul will help with arrangements and translation of the death certificate and other documents.

The *Funeral and Interment Checklist* in the

Appendix separates funerary and interment products and services.

FUNERAL PAYMENT

Excerpts from four samples provided by the Federal Trade Commission's General Price List are given in the *Appendix, Funeral General Price List.* Note that these lists provide places for the prices of all goods and services and for complete service packages, as well as for legal, cemetery, or crematory requirements. Get a price list from two or three local service providers and compare them to these forms to estimate your needs and costs.

Some items that may or may not be found on some General Price Lists include cash-advance items such as flowers, obituary notices, clergy, and organists/soloists. If the exact amount of a cash-advance item is not known, you must receive a good faith estimate. A good faith estimate is a binding contract. Without it, if a cost is misstated or wildly overestimated, it will be difficult to adjust later. Any fees must be disclosed in writing and you must be advised of any refunds, discounts, or rebates on any items you purchase. All reputable establishments will be happy to advise you of all their charges and notify you of any rebates; no disreputable establishment will.

Be conscientious: if you're being charged $800 for a three-line newspaper notice, question it and then question all the other fees. Compare the final charges with those defined in the original contract (or good faith estimate) or on the price list you received before you signed the contract. Question all discrepancies.

Since most of us don't have $10,000 or $12,000 in cash handy, the most common source of funds to cover funeral expenses is an insurance policy. You may purchase a policy for any amount that you think will cover funeral costs (don't forget cash-advance costs) and assign two beneficiaries: the funeral home (not an individual at the funeral home) and your own beneficiary. When the time comes, the policy is given to the funeral director, who processes the claim, and the insurance company sends two checks: one to the funeral home and the remainder, if any, to your beneficiary.

Many independently owned establishments accept the assignment of an insurance policy as payment and most rely on them. There, are, however, some corporate-owned firms that request payment at the time of service. Check with your local provider.

Prepayment Issues. There are many ways other than insurance to pay for funeral expenses. One is to prepay. There are a lot of issues to be considered when prepaying for anything, not the least of which is: Will it be there when I need it? Ask about:

* What protection of prepaid funds is available if

the funeral home or cemetery closes or merges with another?

* How will changes you may wish to make later affect the contract?

* Can you cancel a prepaid contract, are there any cancellation penalties, are all funds returned, or is there a clause that would prohibit a 100% refund? Will the cemetery or entombment owner buy back the property (if you move out of the area)?

* Are contract prices guaranteed? Does the contract also include a statement that defines what will happen if goods and/or services are not available as needed? Will replacement or substitute goods or services be of equal or greater value and is there any cost? How much?

If you're not getting clear, realistic answers to any of the questions, reconsider. Or have your attorney review the contract before you sign. And, of course, never sign anything that you do not understand. This is a big investment—don't throw money away.

FINANCIAL STEPS YOU CAN TAKE

Social Security contributes $255 to funeral expenses and insurance policies may or may not cover all expenses.

Designate a portion of your savings for funeral

expenses or create a **Pay-On-Death** bank account. When establishing a Pay-on-Death account, designate your spouse as a beneficiary on the account. Keep enough funds in the account to live on for three months; that is, enough to carry on paying your bills and for daily living expenses. Insurance benefits will probably be paid within ninety days, but you can always add more to the account as a buffer to protect yourself in case there are any delays. These accounts generate service fees and taxable interest but may be cancelled without penalty and making changes is only a matter of revising forms and is usually free. If your joint funds are frozen at the death of your spouse, you will have a separate account to use until insurance benefits are paid.

Buy a certificate of deposit (CD). A CD earning 5% would almost keep pace with price increases and inflation. Beneficiary changes can be easily made at any time.

Notify family, check with your attorney about any of these arrangements, keep records in your *Life File*, and your attorney should keep copies in their file.

CLOSING AN ESTATE

What an unhappy time this is. The passing of a loved one is trying under any circumstances, and when you have some function to perform regarding their estate, it can be confusing and solemn. You generously offered to help, but now that the time has come you're not exactly sure what needs to be done. So, kind person, we step up to the plate with you.

When a person passes away, all of their possessions become part of their estate. Transferring the estate's assets to beneficiaries is called probate and is supervised by a trustee of the probate court. During probate or summary administration procedures, the court validates the will and the executrix insures that assets are distributed in accordance with your instructions.

If you're helping with an estate for which there is no will, your function may only be to help collect information and find papers. Your job title is "Good Friend," and you have no legal responsibilities.

An executor (male) or executrix (female) is a person named in the will and is responsible for ensuring that all wishes expressed in the will are carried out.

If minor children are involved, a guardian may be named in the will or appointed by the court. A guardian takes on the responsibility for the care of minor children.

If you have been named to any of these jobs, get legal advice immediately. Your attorney or the attorney who wrote the will is the first place to start; their name, address, and phone number will be on the will. You do not have to hire the attorney who wrote the will, but they should be willing to spend some time with you to outline what needs to be done.

Following is a list of items that you should bring to the attorney handling the will:

* A copy of the will;

* insurance and bank account information and access information for safe deposit boxes;

* a copy of the death certificate;

* a list of all assets (and, if possible, the fair market value of each);

* a list of amounts owed to the estate (with names and addresses);

* a list of debts owed by the estate (with names and addresses);

* a list of heirs (spouse and children, parents, siblings, and their children);

* a list of other beneficiaries of the will and their addresses; and the name and address of the deceased's employer.

Get as many of these documents and as much of the information together as possible for the attorney. The attorney will explain the process and any other functions you may have to perform.

Other Issues. Right now you're probably just concerned with the next few hours or days and adjusting to life without your loved one. But financial matters have a limited grace period and very soon you'll be confronted with some simple or complex issues depending on your situation.

You do not have to confront all financial issues immediately or all at once; you do have to relax and take one step at a time. Rushing into decisions now without knowing the consequences is rolling the dice. The choices you and your spouse made may not necessarily be the best ones for you in altered circumstances. Do your homework before making any decisions.

Making decisions under stress is the worst possible time. Do not be pressured by anyone. This cannot be emphasized too strongly or too often. If someone calls insisting on an immediate decision, just tell them that you have to go because someone's at the door; you will comply with their regulations in a timely manner, but you will not be rushed into decisions that are convenient for them. You are the customer and they are only in business to serve you. Some decisions and actions can be put off until after you've gotten professional advice; others are more immediate. Let's sort them out.

Banks and other financial institutions. The first thing you need is access to cash. If it's not in your personal bank account, you can't access it. Don't be surprised by this; unless it's under the mattress or in your own checking account, it's going to take some documentation to prove the money is yours. You do not automatically inherit the funds in a joint account. Banks freeze the funds in joint accounts until they get a certified death certificate, although they may allow access to limited funds for daily use. (That's why you need several copies of the death certificate from the funeral director; one for each bank, insurance company, or other benefits organization, and they will be needed by state and local officials to change names on titles and deeds.) Until the funds are transferred to your name, you will not be able to endorse or deposit checks made out to the joint owner.

Asset management. The same restrictions as just mentioned apply to jointly held assets; you will have only limited authority to sell or manage property. You may wish to consider a nondurable power of attorney for finance naming your spouse as agent.

Following is a list of items you'll need to have on hand within the first month to sixty days.

Immediately-30 days:
- Social Security number
- Veteran's records
- Copies of any wills and/or Letters of Instruction
- Insurance policies
- Bank and/or brokerage accounts, pension plans
- Any pre-paid funeral contracts
- Any powers of attorney

Any credit cards

Thirty to sixty days:
  Medicare/Medicaid information
  Personal and business tax returns
  Mortgages, liens, deeds, car title(s)
  Loan agreements or contracts

The next chapter looks at retirement and budget issues. Retirement and budgets may not seem to be the most intuitive couple, but, in a sense, all retirees are starting over. To adjust to a new income level it seems appropriate to begin with an analysis of what you have and what you can expect to have. It's really not a giant leap, but it is an adjustment and you may have to make other adjustments in daily living habits.

CHAPTER 6: *Retirement*

YOUR CHOICE: BLISS OR BOREDOM

Balmy breezes, warm sun, dazzlingly white sand, and azure seas. The gurgle of a clear mountain stream among stately pines. Bustling through an airport to fly to a destination only dreamt about. The sonorous blast of a horn signaling the departure of a great ship. Does the very word "retirement" conjure such images?

Some of us will realize those dreams; others will be content to tend their backyard gardens during retirement; and yet others will still be working long after retirement. No matter what your circumstances and however you envision the "golden years," you can improve how that time of life plays out.

How much R&R (rest and recuperation) will you need when you retire? A month, a year, two years? What projects have you been thinking about completing during retirement? How long will they take to accomplish? Won't it be nice to be with your spouse 24/7? Perhaps you can suggest some new and innovative way to run the household. How welcome will that be? What social activities are you planning?

We spend many years planning for and anticipating our well-deserved retirement, yet, oddly, most of us don't have the foggiest idea of how we will spend it. Beyond a trip or two, a home-renovation project, or some other wish fulfillment, there are many, many hours in the day to fill. For others, a new job may be a necessity and retirement will be somewhat less complicated.

Years of employment have motivated us each day to face challenges at work, interact with co-workers, generate a product or service, and socialize. When motivation, challenge, interaction, and socialization are removed from the delicate equation that is our retirement life, it's a shock. Finally left to our own devices may not be as idyllic as we had hoped.

Planning for this new phase of life that, statistically, will last more than fifteen years, is more complicated than saving money. Well before you turn in your company ID you should begin planning some long-term activities. As 25 million Baby Boomers retire, there will be a dramatic increase in volunteerism, internet activity, and special interest groups. Plan to be a part of them because the alternates (isolation, depression, lack of motivation) are probably not what you have in mind.

The available material on Social Security, Supplemental Security Income (SSI), Veterans

Benefits, and pensions is (no surprise) chock-a-block full of exceptions, and breaking each down to manageable, small packets is for another book. In the meantime, basic information will get you started.

When you retire, you will be offered a **Spousal consent form** that allows your spouse to receive your pension benefits if you die before your spouse. Your spouse is usually entitled to **survivor's benefits** but not without a signed spousal consent form. Signing a spousal consent form designates that upon your death, any benefits continue to be paid to your spouse; without it, benefits will lapse. It is important to remember that, statistically, wives are more likely to outlive husbands and therefore need more income for a longer retirement. The last chance you have to make sure that your spouse receives survivor's benefits is at the time of your retirement.

SOCIAL SECURITY

For many Americans (about 60%), Social Security represents half or more of their retirement income. During their earning years, they've paid taxes to the Social Security system, and when retirement age arrives, the Social Security Administration (SSA) calculates the benefits they've accrued.

The SSA website invites you to calculate future benefits and offers a simple calculator that will give you a ballpark figure. The SSA mails annual benefits estimates to participants, but if you haven't kept your address up-to-date with them, you may not be receiving it. Order one through their website: www.ssa.gov. At the same time, correct the information they have on file.

Benefits for disabilities are calculated differently, and visiting a local Social Security office is an efficient way of defining your situation and finding information.

To qualify for benefits, you must have worked and earned at least 40 Social Security credits during your working career at a rate of four credits per year. Credits are based on earnings; in 2008, for example, you received one credit for every $1,050 earned. If you earn $4,200 ($1,050 x 4) in 2008, you will have earned the maximum number of 2008 Social Security credits to have 2008 earnings included in your retirement benefits calculation. A contributor can receive partial retirement benefits at age 62 ("early" retirement benefits are about 20% lower than full benefits) or full benefits at age 66 if you were born in 1943 (the date for full retirement gradually increases to age 67 for people born in 1960 or later).

If you continue to work after retirement age and do not apply for benefits, you earn delayed retirement credits. Delayed credits (from a total of 5.5% to 8%) depend on how many months you delay applying for benefits and are based on the amount of money you would have received at retirement age. Remember, however, that these percentages are moving targets; they are recalculated annually and legislation impacts the amounts of all benefits.

SOCIAL SECURITY EARNING LIMITS

When you begin receiving Social Security benefits, you may continue to earn wages, but there are limits on how much you can earn before benefits begin to decrease if you are not at retirement age. If you are at or above retirement age and apply for and receive Social Security benefits, there is not limit on the amount you can earn and no penalty on earnings. The Social Security Administration revises earning limits every year. When they review earnings, they only consider income from wages and self-employment; they do not consider income from pensions, interest on bank accounts, or investment returns. Earning more in a year than the limit amount reduces Social Security benefits by approximately $1 for every $2 earned (if you retire early), and $1 for every $3 earned (if you retire at full retirement age).

Some Social Security benefits are taxable. Taxes are calculated based on age, marital status, earnings, and tax rates are updated annually. Check with your local Social Security office and the following summary of benefits and taxes, reprinted from the U.S. government's Social Security Administration's website, may be helpful.

This update provides new information for 2008 for many items such as Social Security taxes and benefits. By law, these numbers change automatically each year to keep the program up-to-date with increases in price and wage levels. Whether you are working or you are already getting Social Security benefits, these changes are important to you.

Information for people who are working

SOCIAL SECURITY AND MEDICARE TAXES		
Social Security Taxes	2007	2008
Employee/employer (each)	6.2% on earnings up to $97,500	6.2% on earnings up to $102,000
Self-employed *Can be offset by income tax provisions	12.4%* on earnings up to $97,500	12.4%* on earnings up to $102,00

Medicare Taxes	2007	2008
Employee/employer (each)	1.45% on all earnings	1.45% on all earnings

Medicare Taxes	2007	2008
Self-employed *Can be offset by income tax provisions	2.9%* on all earnings	2.9%* on all earnings

Work credits--When you work, you earn credits toward Social Security benefits. You need a certain number of credits to be eligible for Social Security benefits. The number you need depends on your age and the type of benefit for which you are applying. You can earn a maximum of four credits each year. Most people need 40 credits to qualify for retirement benefits.

	2007	2008
	$1000 earns one credit	$1,050 earns one credit

SUSAN M. BIGLIONE & MARTHA E. LAISNE

Information for people who receive Social Security benefits

Earnings Limits

Under federal law, people who are receiving Social Security benefits who have not reached full retirement age are entitled to receive all of their benefits as long as their earnings are under the limits indicated below. For people born in 1943, the full retirement age is 66. The full retirement age will increase gradually each year until it reaches age 67 for people born in 1960 or later.

	2007	2008
At full retirement age or older	No limit on earnings	No limit on earnings
Under full retirement age	$12,960 / For every $2 over the limit, $1 is withheld from benefits.	$13,560 / For every $2 over the limit, $1 is withheld from benefits.
In the year you reach full retirement age	$34,440 / For every $3 over the limit, $1 is with-held from benefits until the month you reach full retirement age.	$36,120 / For every $3 over the limit, $1 is withheld from benefits until the month you reach full retirement age.

Disability Beneficiaries' earnings limits:

If you work while receiving disability benefits you must tell us about your earnings no matter how little you earn. You may have unlimited earnings during a trial work period of up to nine months (not necessarily in a row) and still receive full benefits. Once you have completed your nine-month trial work period, we will determine if you are still entitled to disability benefits. You also may be eligible for other work incentives to help you make the transition back to work.

	2007	2008
Substantial Gainful Activity (Non-blind)	$900 per month	$940 per month
Substantial Gainful Activity (Blind)	$1,500 per month	$1,570 per month
Trial work period month	$640 per month	$670 per month

Information for people who receive Supplemental Security Income (SSI)

Monthly federal SSI payment (maximum)		
	2007	2008
Individual	$623	$637
Couple	$934	$956

Monthly Income Limits		
	2007	2008
Individual whose income is only from wages	$1,331	$1,359
Individual whose income is not from wages	$643	$657
Couple whose income is only from wages	$1,953	$1,997
Couple whose income is not from wages	$954	$976

NOTE: If you have income, your monthly benefit generally will be lower than the maximum federal SSI payment. Remember, you must report all of your income to us. Some states add money to the federal SSI payment. If you live in one of these states, you may qualify for a higher payment. Your income can be greater than the limits indicated and you still may qualify.

Information for people on Medicare

Most Medicare costs are increasing this year to keep up with the rise in health care costs.

	2007	2008
HOSPITAL INSURANCE (PART A)		
For first 60 days in a hospital, patient pays	$992	$1024
For 61st through 90th days in a hospital, patient pays	$248 per day	$256 per day
Beyond 90 days in a hospital, patient pays (for up to 60 more days)	$496 per day	$512 per day
For first 20 days in a skilled nursing facility, patient pays	$0	$0
For 21st through 100th days in a skilled nursing facility, patient pays	$124 per day	$128 per day
PART A PREMIUM BUY-IN: The amount of the premium you pay to buy Medicare Part A depends on the number of Social Security credits you have earned. If you have:		
40 Credits	$0	$0
30-39 Credits	$226 per month	$233 per month
less than 30 Credits	$410 per month	$423 per month

Medical Insurance (Part B)		
Premium	$93.50 per month	$96.40 per month
Deductible	$131 per month	$135 per month

Social Security benefits continue during your lifetime. A spouse may receive up to half of a retired or a disabled worker's benefits while the worker is still alive. To qualify for benefits based on a former spouse's earnings, these general guidelines apply:

- you must have been married at least ten years;
- you and your ex-spouse must both be at least 62 years old;
- checks can't start until two years after a divorce;
- your social security benefit will generally be 50% of your former spouse's.

If your ex-spouse remarries, your benefits are not affected. But if you remarry, you lose the right to benefits based on your former spouse's earnings. If your ex-husband dies, your benefit payments will double; as a divorced widow, you are eligible for 100% of your ex-husband's benefit. If you are thinking of divorce, remember that a divorce one day short of the ten-year requirement will wipe out your right to any of your ex-spouse's social security benefits.

Benefits are not automatic; you can apply at a local

office or online at www.ssa.gov, www.socialsecurity.gov, or by calling 1–800–772–1213. When applying in person, you will have to provide your Social Security card, birth certificate, and proof of U.S. citizenship (and there are other documents that may be required depending on the type of benefits for which you are applying).

You can get a copy of the comprehensive booklet *Social Security Retirement Benefits* (publication 05–10035) from your local Social Security office, or download it from www.ssa.gov/pubs/10035.html, or by calling 1–800–772–1213.

SUPPLEMENTAL SOCIAL SECURITY INCOME (SSI)

Supplemental Social Security Income (SSI) is for individuals with limited incomes and resources. Eligible persons may receive both SSI and Social Security benefits (contact your state office or the Agency of Aging), and income limits vary by state (call 1–800–772–1213 for annual amounts by state). In most states, SSI recipients are automatically eligible for Medicaid. To qualify for SSI you must be a U.S. citizen, 65 years of age or older, or blind or disabled, and individual cash and/or savings cannot exceed $2,000 ($3,000 for couples). Other restrictions apply; for more information, visit the website (www.ssa.gov) or your local Social Security office.

Since SSI benefits are administered by states, the amount of SSI benefits depends on where you live. Base SSI benefits effective 2008 are \$627/month for individuals and \$956/month for couples. SSI is intended to supplement benefits or monthly income, and benefits are periodically reviewed and/or adjusted.

Disability benefits under Social Security and Supplemental Security Income are for people who can no longer work because of physical or mental impairment. Eligibility requirements are based on age, previous earnings, and are calculated differently than are Social Security benefits. Applicants must provide extensive medical documentation, and the disability must be severe enough to prevent them from working for at least a year. It can take up to a year to get an eligibility decision and to begin receiving payments. Contact your local Social Security office, www.ssa.gov, or call 1–800–772–1213 for more information.

VETERANS BENEFITS

Veterans their dependents, and survivors are eligible for benefits from the Department of Veterans Affairs (VA). The VA offers a full range of health care services through more than 150 medical centers, 170 hospitals, and 200 clinics. Life insurance, burial benefits, and various educational, training, and employment programs are available. Their website is: www.va.gov.

Veterans are eligible for benefits if they performed active service and received an honorable or general discharge. Benefits for veterans and their immediate families are determined by service history, disability (and whether or not a disability is related to military service), income, and the size of the household. You may be eligible for some of the following.

Service-related disability compensation. **Service-related disability compensation** is paid monthly and depends on the disability or disease developed or aggravated during service. The amount of compensation is based on the effects and severity of the disability and number of dependents. Benefits are available to dependents and also rely on the nature and severity of the disability and the number of dependents.

Disability pension. **Disability pension** benefits are for wartime veterans completely and/or permanently disabled who meet income restrictions. Veterans must have had at least ninety days of active service with at least one day served during wartime. Spouses and unmarried children may also be eligible. Pension payments vary depending on health care needs and the number of dependents.

Survivors benefits. Survivors of veterans who died because of military-related disabilities may be entitled to **Dependency and Indemnity Compensation**

(DIC) payments. DIC benefits may also be available if the veteran's death was not the direct result of a service-related disability. DIC benefits are linked to the date of a veteran's death (before or after January 1, 1993), military pay grade, marital status, and the number and age of dependent children. Spousal benefits end when the (female) spouse remarries.

Improved Pension Program (IPP). IPP is a survivor's pension fund for death and disabilities that depends on need, family size, and other factors and is intended to supplement other benefits.

Veteran's Health Care Benefits The VA provides a comprehensive range of medical benefits including outpatient services, hospitalization, nursing home and respite care, long-term care, dental, and hearing and vision aids. Some veterans are automatically eligible.

Outpatient medical care is available to all qualified (honorably or generally discharged) veterans with service-related disabilities. Other veterans, as well as survivors and dependents, may be entitled to outpatient services with a co-payment.

Most veterans must apply for benefits, but service-connected veterans are eligible for treatment of service-connected disabilities without enrolling. Veterans may apply for enrollment at any time by calling 1–800–827–1000 or visiting www.va.gov/healtheligibility.

When seeking medical assistance at a VA facility, veterans should be prepared to provide information on their annual income and net worth to determine if they are above or below the Means Test threshold (also referred to as a geographic financial assessment). A Means Test is an annual measure of household income and assets, including spouse and dependent children's income in various geographic areas. For information see www.va.gov/healtheligibility or call 1–800–827–1000.

When applying for medical care, veterans must provide information on their and their spouse's current health insurance coverage. Independent insurance does not affect eligibility, but the VA is required to bill health insurance providers for non-service connected medical care. If the Veterans Administration is unable to collect from a private insurer, they will not bill the veteran or their family.

CHAMPVA, the VA Civilian Health and Medical Program, shares the cost of medical care for veterans' dependents and survivors if they are not eligible for TRICARE (the medical program for civilian dependents provided by the Department of Defense) or Medicare, Part A. For more information, call 1–800–827–1000 or visit www.va.gov.

Women are eligible for the same benefits as male veterans. Services for women also include breast and pelvic examinations and general reproductive health care services, except *in vitro* fertilization; preventive health care includes counseling, contraceptive services, menopause management, Pap smears, and mammography. VA health care professionals provide counseling and treatment to help women overcome psychological trauma resulting from personal and sexual assault during military service and any injury, illness, or psychological condition resulting from such trauma. Women Veterans Coordinators are available at all VA facilities to assist women seeking treatment and/or benefits. VA medical centers have made great strides to ensure privacy for women.

For all veterans, if the VA is unable to provide appropriate services, referrals are made to private practitioners.

Interment benefits. Veterans who received an honorable or general discharge are entitled to burial in a VA cemetery, a burial allowance, as well as a headstone or marker. (See the section entitled *Veterans* in *Chapter 5.*)

PENSIONS

All pension plan providers offer a summary describing the rules of the plan and any event that would trigger distributions (termination, disability, or early retirement). They clearly define how much a contributor will receive at retirement and when payments will be made. If you do not have this vital information, request it from your employer or your spouse's employer and read it carefully. It should be written in clear, concise language, but if you don't understand it, make a list of discussion topics and call the Benefits office.

Following are some common definitions that may be useful to understanding pensions.

Vesting. Most employers require that employees reach some number of months or years of service before they are entitled to participate in pension plans. **Vesting** (or joining the pension plan) occurs when the employee completes that period of service.

Qualified joint and survivor option   An option that extends benefit payments of between 50% and 100% of the original benefits to a surviving spouse. The point is to safeguard the money paid in by assuring that your spouse receives whatever you do not. Without the qualified joint and survivor option, payments would stop at the death of the pensioner.

Annuities were described in *Chapter 2, Finance.* There are other forms of annuities and each has a different conversion option and tax consequence. Check with a professional. Among the most common are *deferred* and *lifetime* annuities.

Deferred annuity   Usually purchased by employees to enhance retirement savings. The appeal of a deferred annuity is its tax implications. When you buy an annuity, you do not pay taxes. Taxes are imposed when the annuity is redeemed. The life-span or term of an annuity is, therefore, an important consideration (taxes can be deferred for many years). For example, you may buy deferred annuities during your earning years and save them for retirement (or any other time you wish); when you retire you get the principal and any earnings. When you withdraw the money is when you pay any taxes.

Lifetime annuity. A lifetime annuity provides payments for the rest of your life. Individuals nearing retirement and those already retired usually purchase income annuities with their savings, or they may be purchased by making periodic payments during your working years. In exchange for its cost, the insurer guarantees regular income for the rest of the life of the purchaser. Money received from an annuity generally supplements other income. Payments are fixed (predetermined amounts) or variable (different amounts depending on the current interest rate). This type of annuity is not cheap: a quick calculation reveals that a $10,000 annuity might return $59 a month while a $100,000 annuity might return $593 a month.

Defined contribution plan Defined contribution pension plan benefits are based on the amount contributed and are affected by plan income, management expenses (something to watch), and plan gains and losses. Examples of defined contribution plans are 401(k)s, employee stock ownership plans, profit sharing plans, and money purchase plans. Participants are required to make some investment decisions. See the earlier discussion regarding investment decisions in *Chapter 2, Finance,* at *Pension/Retirement Plans, 401(k).*

Money purchase plan. A plan to which employer contributions are fixed; employers may contribute up to 25% of an employees' compensation.

Defined benefit plan. A defined benefit plan provides a specific monthly benefit at retirement. Benefits may be calculated considering participants' salary and length of service. Private sector (industry) plans may not require employee contributions but most public sector (government) plans do. Participants are usually not required to make investment decisions.

Money purchase plans and defined benefit plans set retirement age and eligibility guidelines. They may allow early retirement, and benefits may be paid upon termination or in case of disability. Benefits must also be convertible to a lifetime annuity (see above). If you are married, your benefits must be available in the form of a qualified joint and survivor annuity (see above).

A 401(k) plan allows you to take some or all of your vested accrued benefits when you reach age 59½, retire, become disabled, terminate, or suffer hardship. 401(k)s are very flexible. Review the investments in a 401(k); consider the mix of stocks and bonds in it to be sure that it will achieve your financial goals.

Profit-sharing plan or **stock bonus plan** Most plans allow for benefits to be received at retirement, after a specified number of years of employment (see *vesting* above), or when you become disabled, or terminate your employment. The plan terms may contain other perks or restrictions. Check with your employer's Benefits Officer.

The terms of a pension plan dictate its benefits. If you are covered under a defined contribution plan, it may pay a single lump sum or some other way. Some plans offer a life annuity and joint and survivor options. Be smart; do your research.

BUDGETING

Almost no one likes the word, and fewer like to do it. Be positive: chuck that offensive word out of your vocabulary and think in terms of power: the power to control your destiny, the power to make knowledgeable decisions, the power of self-reliance and self-confidence. If you know all about what has already been discussed, you're a Master of your Universe. If not, information may be all you need. There's plenty of it available and it's not difficult to find (the internet, a banker, friend, relative, courses at a local college or high school, the U.S. Treasury department, the Benefits Office at your employment). The "buyer beware" caveat applies of course: each source may have their own agenda; an investment broker may want you to invest 80% of your discretionary (extra) income in investments they suggest; a banker may suggest that an equity or some other type of loan will solve your problems; and a friend or relative may think you're living either too high or too low on the hog.

Self-reliance is the way to go. Only you know the questions that are appropriate to your situation. And since there really are very few people who want to know every last detail of, say, an insurance policy, and chances are you're not one of them, you need to clearly frame the questions you must have answered. If you've been surprised by anything you've read so far, you appreciate how important it is to understand the basics. "I need to make my money go further," is too vague; "I'm not going to have any more $5 lattes," is not right either; it may be the only time you treat yourself in a busy day or week and you deserve it. This is not an exercise in self-denial. Find the middle ground.

Money is a tool: you have it or you don't; you owe it or you don't; it's working for you or it isn't; and you're using it wisely or not. If you don't know what's in your checking account, mutual fund, or savings account at this very moment (no guesses), you're not in control. If you don't know what your bills will be next month, and if anything comes up between now and then, you may not, you're risking falling behind or a lot worse.

There's nothing new here; we've all heard it before. But now it's time to do something about it. No more putting it off. If you don't have the time, make it. Make the power happen!

First, get it all out on the table. Following is a general budget form. Just plug in good guesses because all you want to do now is get a rough idea of where you stand (that's all a budget is, anyway, a snapshot of your financial condition at this very moment). Review the bottom line and then go back and look for places that you can adjust (or at least modify) that are not too painful or unpleasant (turning off the heat in January is a bad idea).

Then think about creating a budget that has the flexibility to accommodate life and life's unexpected events. Never create a budget you can't live with: *big* waste of time. Flexibility is key. Life happens, and a small extra expense is not going to make all your budgeting efforts useless. Make it up somewhere else. Budgeting isn't an exercise in penance—it is an exercise in control. Even if you don't create a personal budget, if you fill in the numbers on the form you may be surprised at where your money is going and may think that one of the five-dollar bills you're spending on a latte may be better spent on increasing your savings, building a personal slush fund, or saving for a vacation. The bottom line is making your dollars work just as hard for you as you did for them. If you don't remember what you spent $50 or $100 on last month, that's $50 or $100 that's lost unless you charged it, of course; in which case you'll probably pay almost 25% interest on it for a long time.

CONTROL—GET IT AND KEEP IT!

In the form below, use monthly amounts; if you pay something quarterly, divide the payment by 4.

	Cost	Subtotal	Totals
Rent	$		
Mortgage	$		
Property tax	$		
Homeowners Insurance	$		
Condo Fee			
		$	
Electric	$		

Gas	$	
Oil	$	
Butane	$	
Heat	$	
Water/Sewer	$	
		$	
Child Care	$	
Child Support	$	
		$	
Groceries	$	
Lunches	$	
Eating Out	$	
Clothing	$	
Clothes Cleaning Repair	$	

		$	
Medical/Other Insurance	$		
Physicians	$		
Optometrist	$		
Dentist	$		
Hospital	$		
Drugs	$		
		$	
Car Payment	$		
Car Insurance	$		
Car Maintenance Repair	$		
Public Transportation	$		
Gas	$		
		$	

Phone (landline)	$		
Cell Phone	$		
Pager	$		
Cable/Disk TV	$		
Internet Connection	$		
Modem Rental	$		
		$	
Household Maintenance	$		
Student Loans	$		
Tuition	$		
Other Loans	$		
Credit Card 1 (include annual fee)	$		
Credit Card 2 (include annual fee)	$		

Credit Card 3 (is this one necessary?)	$		
Credit Card 4 (is this one necessary?)	$		
Health/Personal Care	$		
Veterinary/Pet Care	$		
		$	
Books/Supplies	$		
Memberships Dues	$		
Crafts/Sports	$		
		$	
Savings	$		
Retirement Savings	$		
Emergency Fund Savings	$		
Donations	$		

Entertainment: Lessons	$		
Movies/Concerts	$		
Gym	$		
Clubs	$		
		$	
Landscaping	$		
Pool Maintenance	$		
Travel	$		
Add all subtotals		$	
All income			$
Minus total subtotals			$
What you have to play with ("discretionary" income):			$

Well done! This is a big step in gaining control of your life and building personal and financial strength. Stop now and take a breather, the hard work is done.

Now let's look at where cuts can be made that aren't going to be as painful as you might think, starting with housing expenses. There probably isn't much you can do as a renter except control heating and air conditioning costs. Get a programmable heat/AC control; they really do pay for themselves very quickly.

If you have a mortgage, you have options. Is it an Adjustable Rate Mortgage (ARM) or a fixed-rate mortgage?

Following are simple example numbers: assume a $200,000 mortgage at 5% for 30 years.

With a fixed rate mortgage your monthly payment is $1,073.64. Over the life of the loan you will pay $186,511.00 in interest for a total payoff of $386,511. Comparing that to an **Adjustable Rate Mortgage** (ARM) that, over the life of the loan interest may be increased (several times) by a quarter of 1% (.025) for a total of as much as 2% a year (and the likelihood of it decreasing are in negative numbers), you will pay $197,586.67 in interest (without any increase in the rate) for a total payoff of $397,586.67. That's a difference of $11,075. Can you think of a way to spend $11,075 other than giving it to a bank?

If you're thinking about converting to an interest only loan, think about this: it's exactly what is says it is. You only make the interest payments; at the end of the loan you owe the principal. (From our example, for a loan of $200,000 you'll owe $200,000 at the end of thirty years.) Enough said.

A **reverse mortgage** is for homeowners aged 62 or older who wish to borrow against the equity in their homes. It pays the homeowner a line of credit, lump sum, or series of monthly payments. The homeowner does not repay the loan as long as they live in the home. The loan is repaid when the owner sells the home or dies. The estate repays the mortgage with proceeds from the sale of the home or with other funds. For more information, visit AARP's website at www.aarp.org and search *reverse mortgage*).

Get professional advice if you're thinking about refinancing.

Are you paying Private Mortgage Insurance (PMI)? **Private Mortgage Insurance** is a policy for the lender (that you buy) that guarantees that you will repay the loan. After you have paid 20% of the principal of the original loan, in our example, $40,000, the bank feels that you will continue to pay and will likely repay the entire amount, so they cancel the Private Mortgage Insurance policy. PMI is usually a half of one percent of the loan (in our example $200,000–$20,000 down = $180,000;

$180,000 x .005 = $900 per year; or $75 per month). If you have paid 20% of your mortgage, you should not be paying PMI. Banks are responsible for canceling PMI, but you should check.

Statement timing. An often overlooked aspect of bill paying is when you get your statement. Your energy utility provider, bank, or credit card lender sends you a bill demanding payment on a date that is at their convenience. That's fine for them, but it may not be fine for you if their payment date is not in sync with your paycheck. The result is that you may be late making your payments; their computers will mark you as a late payer, which will trigger a late fee and wreck your credit. Call these companies and demand that they change your payment due date to one that is convenient for you. If you don't get satisfaction from the first person you talk to, move up the chain by asking to speak to their supervisor. If the supervisor can't help, ask to speak to their supervisor (utilities and credit card companies have an endless supply of supervisors, keep going until the date is changed). Demand service.

Electricity and home fuel. There are many ways to conserve on these power sources. Get a programmable heat and air conditioning thermostat. They cost about $50, you can install them yourself, and they will control the heating and cooling while you are not at home and at night. Don't worry about the cat; it's wearing fur and is too bone idle to work up a sweat.

When was the last time you had your furnace serviced? Most energy companies offer energy-saver deals, check with your provider. Log on to www.eere.energy.gov and click on *Consumers* for more tips. A new type of water heater available heats the water on demand, not all-day long; they are a tenth of the size of an ordinary water tank, and there is an energy tax break for installation.

Phones. Analyze your usage and get a grip on it. Figure out what your minute requirements are and don't pay for what you are not using; if you're not using all your minutes every month, consider another plan that lets you carry over unused minutes. Review your contract every other year to keep up with all the new deals that are offered. Consider buying a new phone with enhanced services (enhanced 911 and GPS that allows emergency operators to track your location). Compare prices online. If you decide to cancel your current plan, be sure you know when to cancel; if you don't give some providers thirty days' notice before the end of the contract, they automatically renew it and there are large fees for canceling an existing contract at other times.

Food and clothing. If you prepare your own food, you can save scads of money. It's as simple as that. If you are spending $10 a day for lunch, bringing a prepared meal three days a month will pay for the monthly charge of a basic landline telephone. Reduce your spending on clothes. While we all want to be up-to-date, sometimes we have to compromise. Compromise is good.

Transportation. Have you reviewed your car insurance policy recently? Check rates (and complaints) online at your state's department of insurance. Find out if you are eligible for a good-driver discount. Or, if you've taken defensive driver training, you may be eligible for a discount. Investigate municipal transportation fee options; some cities offer reduced rates for consistent usage of public transportation, and insurance companies offer lower auto insurance rates for taking public transportation. If you're driving less, your insurer may offer a low-mileage rate discount. Have you moved to a safer area? Insurers consider your home location when calculating premiums. And remember that all these insurers check your credit rating. If you've cleared up any credit card score problems or they've improved over time, ask your insurer to review your account.

Homeowners insurance. Have you reviewed this policy lately? If your situation has changed, your policy should reflect the change. Call your agent and ask if there are any discounts. If you have had the policy for some time (more than six years) or reached retirement age, you may be eligible for a discount. You might find the Insurance Information Institute's website helpful: www.iii.org. If you have moved into an area with fewer crimes, you may be eligible for lower rates. Also go to the Life and Health Insurance Foundation for Education's website to see what policies are available and to calculate what you need (www.life-line.org).

Monthly debts. Please read the section on credit cards and get rid of them as fast as you can. You will never be out of debt as long as you have a credit card. Cut up any credit cards you have that have an annual fee. Pay off the highest interest rate cards. Avoid late charges. Get all the credit cards out of your purse or wallet, write down their names, account numbers, minimum payment amounts, totals due, and the company telephone number (if you haven't already done this and filed it in your ***Life File***). Choose one to keep. Make sure it does not have an annual fee. Now call each company and cancel the cards. Ask about stopping all interest on remaining balances or reducing the interest rate. Make sure that the account is marked "closed at customer's request" when it is reported to credit rating services (and send a confirming letter to each credit bureau). If you don't, the credit rating bureaus assume the issuer called in the card and that adversely affects your credit. If your credit rating has improved call the credit card companies and ask them to review your new situation and ask for an interest-rate reduction.

Eating out. Don't stop, just don't do it as often. It takes some time and thought, but if you prepare foods in advance you'll be stunned at how much you can save. Instead of going out three times a week, cut back to once a week. Takeout is very expensive. A real saving.

Incidentals. Incidentals might include that high-priced coffee you pick up in the morning (multiply its cost by 20 and figure out what monthly bill you could pay with that money) and impulse buying. When you go to any store, have a list of items you want to purchase in hand and don't buy anything else. Wandering around a mall or store is a recipe for credit card disaster. Think about the value of an item. If this is a new concept, you'll be amazed at how much less you'll be tempted to buy based on value.

Restraint and discipline should become part of your decision-making process for all purchases. Restraint: Do I really need this?; discipline: If I wait a month will I be able to buy it without using a credit card. You don't have to restrain and discipline yourself for every purchase, but start; soon enough they will become a part of all your decision making.

Review all your memberships; if you're not using them, why are you paying for them? See if your gym offers a month-to-month or per-day membership. The same applies to newspaper and magazine subscriptions; if you're not reading them, cancel them.

Checking account. Is it interest bearing? Check out the various online options that are currently paying higher interest. If you opened your account years ago with a minimum balance, there's more than likely a better deal available now. If it's an account that you've had for a very long time, you're probably paying charges and fees for which newer accounts are no longer charged (check writing, for example). Some accounts are free with direct deposit. But watch the other fees; if banks are giving you something "free," you can be sure they'll make it up in overdraft fees, cash-advance fees, or somewhere else.

Utilities. Get utility companies to change their payment due dates to dates that accommodate your financial schedule, not theirs. If they charge late fees, they should be willing to offer you the opportunity to at least avoid them. If you haven't updated your computer service in a while, now is a good time. Some ISP providers offer combined computer/telephone service that may be cheaper than what you're using. Check out the deal carefully, especially offers that expire in three or six months. If you're renting a modem, unless there's a really good reason not to, buy your own; they cost less than $100.

Now look for old money. If you've changed jobs in the last three months, call former employers and ask about pensions, 401(k)s, employee savings, health savings, or flexible spending accounts, and any other funds you may have left behind.

Take your last three years of income tax returns to a reputable tax service. Ask if they'll review them to see if they could have done better. If they can get back more than the service will cost, go for it.

Take advantage of free money. If your employer matches or adds a percent of your contribution to a 401(k) or mutual fund, try to contribute as much as you can and at least enough for your employer to match.

Some brokerage houses and mutual funds have high, and sometimes hidden, transaction fees; do your research and find reputable institutions that do not.

Have you ever been on a treasure hunt? Do you own a savings bond or a registered Treasury note or bond that has matured and is no longer earning interest? Or a savings bond that you haven't received in the mail? Check out Treasure Hunt at www. treasurydirect.gov (go to *Individual, Tools,* then *Treasure Hunt*).

Promptly use store gift certificates. If the expiration date has passed the store is not obligated to honor them.

When you pay off a debt, continue to pay that amount to yourself for savings, a vacation, or a personal treat. Budget for a fun item (vacation or toy—adult or child). Don't include too many expense items in your budget, just actual expenses. But make savings an expense item; pay your savings account as if it were a bill.

Set aside some money each month for items that need to be paid quarterly, semi-annually, or yearly.

Adjust your budget frequently, keep it flexible.

Slow and steady is boring, but it truly does win the race. Now that you've done all this work, use it to your advantage. If the budget reveals that you are not yet the Master of Your Universe, make it so!

Do well, do good, and make it happen for *you!*

Glossary

401(k). A 401(k) plan is an employer-sponsored savings plan. Money you save is tax-deferred; you pay tax only when you start to withdraw funds, which is permitted at age 59½ and required at age 70½. 401(k) funds are professionally managed.

Activities of daily living. The five activities of daily living are: bathing, eating, dressing, toileting, and walking. Consider these activities when purchasing long-term insurance.

Adjustable Rate Mortgage (ARM). The amount of each monthly payment for an adjustable rate mortgage depends on the current interest rate. As interest rates rise or fall, so does your monthly payment. Banks are also allowed to increase the interest rate on an adjustable rate mortgage in increments of ½ of 1% (.005) to up to 2% per year.

Administrator. The person named in a will to carry out the terms of a will. They collect estate property, pay debts, and distribute assets according to the instructions in the will. The court assigns an administrator when none is named in a will.

Adult daycare. A (non-residential) facility for the personal care and supervision of elderly. Provides social, recreational, and health activities designed to improve self-awareness and the level of functioning; may offer meals or snacks, and transportation to and from the facility.

Annuity. An insurance company plan that you may purchase outright or in incremental payments. The insurance company invests the money over the life of the annuity. At the end of the annuity's term, or life, you redeem it for a lump sum or regular payments (usually monthly). Annuity payments may be structured in a variety of ways; for as long as you live or for some specified length of time. Annuity products are complex; consult a professional before purchasing.

Arbitration. Meeting(s) with a professional arbitrator to resolve marital disputes (except child care and custody). An arbitrator may file a binding decision with the court.

Artificial means. Water and nutrition supplied through feeding tubes or other invasive means.

Asset. An asset is any item you own that has a dollar-exchange value. Real assets that can be converted to cash include such things as real estate, cars, boats, or jewelry. Financial assets include bonds, stocks, certificates of deposit, or mutual funds.

Asset allocation funds. Unlike funds for which the terms of the fund define fund activities and mix of investment vehicles, in an asset allocation mutual fund, the fund manager decides what mixture of stocks and bonds are held in the fund. Also referred to as a "diversified fund."

Assisted living and *assisted living facilities.* The services provided fall into two categories: medical and non-medical, and vary at each facility; that is, not all facilities offer the same services. Medical assistance may include health care, social, and recreational activities; assistance with eating, bathing, dressing, toileting, and walking; administering medicine, using eye drops, and transportation. Non-medical assistance may include help with appointments for health care and social services; meal preparation, laundry, reminders to take medications, and transportation. Residential facilities may have private rooms or apartments and communal dining.

Autopsy. A clinical inspection of the human body to determine a person's health during life and cause of death.

Balanced funds. These mutual funds attempt to achieve a balanced mixture of risk, income, and capital appreciation by investing in a combination of bonds and stocks. Unlike an asset allocation fund, investment in each class of asset is restricted by the terms, or objectives, of the fund to achieve maximum benefit for shareholders.

Bankruptcy. The development of a plan to resolve debts either through the division of assets or a managed repayment program. In the most common form, "Liquidation," a trustee of the court collects all the nonexempt property, sells it, and distributes the proceeds to creditors. Other forms help people repay debts over three to five years ("Reorganization") or allow business owners to remain in business and use the revenue to repay creditors.

Basic care. Services required to maintain daily living activities: personal care assistance (eating, dressing, bathing, toileting, and walking), supervision and safety, access to 24-hour emergency care, and social and recreational activities.

Basic insurance plan. Covers hospitalization and related charges.

Bed-hold policy. Sometimes referred to as a "bed reservation." If a care facility resident is hospitalized, nursing homes generally hold their beds for as long as they or their insurance pays for it. Medicare generally covers a maximum of three days of hospitalization. When a Medicare patient's hospitalization exceeds the three-day maximum, they are entitled to be readmitted to the care facility only when a new bed becomes available. Bed-hold policies are regulated in some states.

Beneficiary. A person designated as the recipient of funds or other property under a will, trust, insurance policy, pension plan, or the like.

Benefits period. A Medicare benefit period begins on the first day of hospitalization or entering a skilled nursing facility. In the case of hospitalization, for example, the benefit period ends 60 consecutive days after discharge *and* there were no hospital visits during those sixty days *for the same condition.* A new benefit period begins if you return to the hospital *for any reason* after the first benefit period has ended. You must pay the deductible for each benefit period. There is no limit to the number of Medicare benefit periods.

Blue Cross Blue Shield. A national federation of not-for-profit service insurers that contract with hospitals (Blue Cross) and physicians (Blue Shield) to provide prepaid health care benefits.

Board and care homes (also referred to as group living arrangements). These arrangements are for those unable to live independently but who do not need nursing home services. Most board and care facilities provide help with some activities such as eating, bathing, dressing, and using the bathroom and may provide recreational activities.

Bond. Bonds are referred to as debt instruments. A bond is an IOU issued by corporations, governments, or state municipalities. The issuer agrees to pay back the face value of the bond (known as the principal) after a specified period of time. In return for this "loan," the issuer also agrees to pay a fixed rate of interest to the bondholder during the life, or term, of the bond. Bonds are considered less risky than stocks but are less lucrative.

Bond mutual funds. There are many types of bonds to invest in: at one end of the scale, junk bonds are very high risk, while at the other end government bonds are low risk. Bond funds are subject to interest rate risk; if interest rates go up, the value of the fund goes down.

Casket/Coffin. A container or chest for the sanitary transportation and interment of remains.

Catch-up provision. If you are fifty years old or older, a catch up provision allows you to make additional contributions (above the maximum) each year to 401(k)s, mutual funds, and individual retirement accounts.

Cemetery property. A grave site usually referred to as a "plot."

Certificates of Deposit (CDs). CDs are offered by banks,

brokerages, or thrift institutions; typically generate higher interest than regular savings accounts; and are insured up to $100,000 by FDIC. They are issued in many denominations, for a fixed length of time, at a fixed interest rate. For example, a CD may be issued for $1,000 for six months at 5% interest; at the end of six months the owner receives $1,000 plus 5% interest. CDs are relatively low-risk investments. There are penalties for early redemption; that is, redeeming them before their maturity date.

Chronic illness. Defined as needing substantial assistance with two of the five activities of daily living (bathing, eating, dressing, toileting, walking) or severe cognitive impairment, including Alzheimer's, requiring substantial supervision.

COBRA (Comprehensive Omnibus Budget Reconciliation Act of 1989). This act guarantees group insurance rates when transferring from one employer's group plan to another. It also guarantees minimum, life-sustaining treatment and stabilization procedures for anyone in emergency care whether or not they have insurance. In certain situations, a retired employee, their spouse, and dependent children may be qualified beneficiaries.

Codicil. "Codicil" simply means supplement. In legal terms it means a supplement containing an addition, explanation, or modification to something in a will.

Co-insurance. Not all policies require co-insurance. Like co-payments, they are required for covering services after you have paid the full annual deductible. Co-insurance amounts, however, are not fixed but depend on the cost of the covered service. Co-insurance amounts are generally figured on a ration of 80:20 (the insurer pays 80% and the insured pays 20%). Although they do not differ between policies for a single person or for families, they apply to the primary policy holder and separately to all dependents.

Collaborative divorce. Spouses sign a contract agreeing not to litigate. The couple and their independent lawyers then negotiate a settlement. The agreement is presented to the court and there are no formal court proceedings.

Collateral. Collateral is an asset that you give to a lender to keep until you've repaid a loan. When the loan is repaid, you get the asset back. If you don't repay the loan, the lender may keep your asset, and to get their money back may sell it.

Columbarium. An above-ground structure with niches for urns. It may be outdoors or part of a mausoleum.

Community property. Nine U.S. states have community property laws: Arizona, California, Idaho, Louisiana, Nevada, New Mexico, Texas, Washington, and Wisconsin. Briefly, states define community property as assets acquired by a husband and wife during the course of their marriage using income earned while they are residents of a community property state.

Community services. There are any number and variety of helpful community services available that focus on the needs of the elderly and incapacitated. Some, such as volunteer groups that help with tasks like shopping or transportation, may be free. Others may be available for a fee. The following services may be found locally: adult daycare, meal programs (Meals-on-Wheels), senior centers, bill paying, and visitor programs.

Comprehensive major medical insurance plan. This type of plan is usually a combination of features of medical and surgical insurance plans. It may include some of the features of major medical and catastrophic illness plans.

Continuing care retirement community. Community housing that provides several levels of care based on residents' needs: independent living apartments to skilled nursing care in an affiliated nursing home. "Zoned" for levels of care (individual homes or apartments, assisted living facilities, and nursing homes), residents move from one level of care (or zone) to another within the community.

Co-payment. An insurance cost shared by you and the medical service provider.

Coroner. A coroner is a political appointee, while a medical examiner is a physician (usually a pathologist).

Corporate bonds. Bonds are IOUs issued by corporations to fund acquisitions, research, or expansion and are considered fixed-income securities (that is, they are not directly affected by interest rates or market volatility). Corporate bonds are usually issued for short-term (1–5 years), intermediate-term (5–12 years), or long-term (more than 12 years) investment. They are also referred to as debt instruments, and investing in debt is safer than investing in equity (stocks) because if a corporation goes bankrupt, debtholders are paid before stockholders.

Cremation. Exposing remains to extreme heat and flame as a part of some funeral rites.

Crypt. A space in a mausoleum or other above-ground facility to hold cremated or whole remains.

Custodial care. Non-skilled personal care such as assistance with bathing, dressing, getting in or out of bed or chair, eating, walking, using the toilet, and may also include assistance with minor tasks. Custodial care is usually provided by private nurses or aides.

Death certificate. A legal paper signed by an attending physician showing the cause of death and other vital statistics pertaining to the deceased. Death certificates are filed with federal, state, and local offices by the physician and mortician.

Deductible. An amount of money you pay out of pocket before insurance benefits begin to be paid. Deductible amounts generally start about $250 and go up to more than $1,000. Ordinarily, the higher the deductible, the lower the premium. A high deductible on a life insurance policy is a requirement for participation in a health savings account.

Deferred annuity. Usually purchased from an insurance company to supplement retirement savings. Payments of income, in installments or a lump sum are delayed until the investor elects to receive them and taxes are not paid until funds are withdrawn. A deferred annuity may be converted to an income annuity. A deferred annuity may also provide a death benefit of guaranteed principal and earnings. Annuity products are complex, consult a professional before purchasing.

Defined benefit pension plan. A defined benefit pension plan provides a specific monthly benefit at retirement. Benefits may be calculated considering participants' salary and length of service. Private sector (industry) plans may not require employee contributions but most public sector (government) plans do. Also referred to as a "qualified benefit plan."

Defined contribution pension plan. Defined contribution pension plans are accounts offered by employers who set aside money for employees. The amount contributed is fixed but the benefit is not; that is, the amount of any benefit may be changed at any time by the company. Benefits may be based on the amount contributed and are affected by length of service, plan income, management expenses, and plan gains and loses.

Dependency and indemnity compensation (DIC). Survivors of veterans who died because of military-related disabilities may be entitled to Dependency and Indemnity Compensation payments. DIC benefits may also be available if the veteran's death was not the direct result of a service-related disability.

Dependent. A dependent is a person that a taxpayer claims relies on them for financial support. They may be a spouse, child, stepchild, legally adopted child, or any individual who is under the care and supervision of another person.

Direct burial. Remains are buried shortly after death, usually in a simple container without embalming.

Direct cremation. Cremation occurs shortly after death without embalming.

Disability insurance. Guarantees a monthly income if your ability to work is impaired by illness or injury. Coverage is designed to replace a reasonable percentage of your pre-disability income (ranging from 60%-80%).

Disability pension. Veterans' disability pension benefits are for wartime veterans completely and permanently disabled who meet income restrictions. Veterans must have 90 days of active service, of which at least one day must have been served during wartime.

Disaster Plan. A plan for each member of the family or household to follow in an emergency. Should include meeting places, emergency services telephone numbers, personal contact numbers, and personal medical information.

Discharge planner. This hospital or medical facility person (or department) has a wealth of knowledge about local care facilities, their levels of care and costs, as well as in-depth knowledge of Medicare, Medicaid, and private insurance.

Disinterment. The removal of remains from an interment or entombment site.

Durable power of attorney. Allows you to designate someone to conduct your business. A powerful legal tool.

Durable power of attorney for health care. Allows you to designate someone to make on-the-spot medical decisions on your behalf when you cannot. Your agent may discuss your medical condition, review medical records, but they cannot make financial decisions. May be revoked by you at any time for any reason.

Elder Care Locator. For help finding elder services in your community (1–800–677–1116)

Embalming. A preservation process that may or may not be necessary depending upon the type of funeral arrangements and the circumstances of death.

Emergency medical response system. An alert system that may be purchased, rented, or leased from an emergency medical response provider that is installed in your home. It consists of a wireless radio transmitter worn by the user to contact a monitoring center via a landline telephone. It is generally used by elderly living alone or by those with chronic illnesses.

Endowment care fund. Funds collected with cemetery property purchases and placed in trust for facility maintenance and upkeep. States generally monitor the fund and establish its minimum amount.

Entombment. A term used to express burial when it is in an above-ground columbarium or mausoleum.

Equity fund. A mutual fund for long-term capital growth with some income. There are many types of equity (stock) funds because there are many different types of stocks. Also known as growth funds, these mutual funds often invest in fast-growing companies that frequently reinvest their earnings in expansion, acquisitions, and research.

Estate. One's property or possessions; all that a person owns.

Estate tax. A tax imposed on the net worth of a decedent's property prior to distribution to heirs. It is also referred to as a "death tax."

Eulogy. An oration in honor of the deceased, usually offered at the funeral home, religious site, or interment location.

Executor (male). The person named in a will to carry out the provisions of the will.

Executrix (female). The person named in a will to carry out the provisions of the will.

Extreme (or "extraordinary") means. A term often found in a living will to indicate the use of breathing tubes or other external apparatus to support or replace a vital bodily function that is no longer working.

Fiduciary responsibility. When someone is entrusted with the management of property, or with the power to act on someone's behalf or for their benefit, they have a duty to perform these tasks in the best interests of that person. An executrix or executor of an estate, for example, must make decisions that are in the best interests of the estate. A trustee must make decisions that are in the best interests of the trust.

Fixed income fund. Mutual funds designed to provide fixed periodic payments and eventually return the principal. An example would be a fixed-rate government bond fund.

Fixed rate mortgage. Monthly payments remain the same during the life of the loan. The amount of interest you agree to pay when you sign for the loan is the amount you will be charged over the life of the loan, it does not change. (Compare with Adjustable Rate Mortgages.)

Foreclosure. When collateral (or asset) is given to a lender to keep until a loan is repaid. If the loan is not repaid, the lender may keep the asset or sell it to get their money back. Borrowers receive a notice that the lender intends to foreclose (keep or sell the asset).

Funded trust. To function, a trust must have assets. A funded trust contains money or assets.

General Price List. Funeral directors are required to show or give you a list of all of their products and services, called a General Price List.

Global mutual fund. Global mutual funds invest anywhere in the world.

Grantor. A person who establishes and defines the terms of a trust.

Grave liner. A concrete cover that rests above a casket in a grave. Some liners cover the tops and sides of a casket and minimize ground settling. Some cemeteries require liners while others require vaults.

Group living arrangements (see also Board and Care). Group living arrangements (sometimes referred to as group homes) for those unable to live independently but who do not need nursing home services. Most board and care facilities provide help with some activities of daily living.

Health care proxy. Like a power of attorney for health care but here you identify and/or appoint a proxy agent and define the medical procedures and explain the treatment(s) you wish or do not wish to receive. Your agent is responsible for assuring that this directive is respected and carried out.

Health Reimbursement Account (HRA). A fund into which an employer makes contributions for employees. When an employee submits a claim, the employer pays the health service provider from the fund. HRAs may not be rolled over.

Health Savings Account (HSA). An individual or employee account to which both employer and/or employee may contribute. Funds are generally used for medical expenses not covered by other policies. HSAs accept investment dividends and may be rolled over.

Home equity. The amount of value you have in your home. When you buy a house, the money you put down is your initial equity. With every mortgage payment you make, the amount of the loan principal decreases and your equity increases. The value of your home equity changes when the value of the property changes. For example, if you buy a house for $100,000 and your down payment is $20,000 (20%), your equity is $20,000. Two weeks later, however, your home is revalued by a local tax assessor to $120,000. While your equity is still $20,000, it no longer represents 20% of the total cost of the home; it now represents 17%. This may seem to be splitting hairs (bankers like to do that), but it is important if you must carry Private Mortgage Insurance (PMI) until your total equity equals 20%.

Home health care. Usually includes visits by licensed nurses, qualified physical, occupational, and speech therapists and home health aides, audiology services, and medical social services by a social worker.

Homestead Exemption laws. A type of protection for a person's residence during bankruptcy.

Hospice care. For terminally ill patients with a life expectancy of less than one year and no reasonable prospect of a cure. Hospice services are designed to ease discomfort during the last phase of life. Hospice facilities specialize in physical care and family counseling; the goal is to care for, not cure, an illness. A team of doctors, nurses, home health aides, and social workers, counselors, and trained volunteers help patients and family cope with illness. Hospice care may be provided at home, at a hospice facility, or at a nursing home.

Hospital indemnity insurance plan. Instead of paying specific hospital charges, indemnity plans pay a specific, fixed-dollar amount per day of hospitalization, no matter what the actual charges are and what other coverage the insured has.

Improved Pension Program (IPP). IPP is a veteran's survivor's pension fund for death and disability that depends on need and is intended to supplement other benefits such as Social Security and Medicare.

Income mutual funds. Mutual funds designed to provide income on a steady basis. These funds invest primarily in utility stocks and nationally recognized, well established, and financially sound companies.

Index mutual funds. These funds are based on the performance of market indices such as the Standard & Poor's 500 or the Russell 2000.

Individual Retirement Account (IRA). A savings plan that may be established at a bank, brokerage house, or credit union. It has a maximum limit on annual contributions. Contributions and earnings accumulate tax free until withdrawn. You may have as many IRAs as you wish and roll-over options are available.

Inpatient. A patient admitted to a hospital or clinic who requires at least one overnight stay.

Intermediate care. Typically care that is medically necessary provided occasionally by licensed professionals under the direct orders of a physician.

Interment. In-ground burial of physical remains or ashes.

International mutual funds. International mutual funds invest only outside their home country.

Intestate. When a person dies without a will. There is a whole set of legal, state, and government regulations that address this situation. When a person leaves no will, the state and government determine heirs and make decisions on estate taxes and assets. "Testate" means having made and left a valid will.

Inurnment. Placing the cremated remains (in an urn) in a mausoleum or columbarium.

Irrevocable trust. Often (but not always) established by a will. An irrevocable trust is an independent entity under the law. Once established, terms may not be changed, it may not be revoked, and assets may not be withdrawn.

Joint ownership. When two or more people own an asset, their rights to it, and their responsibilities for it, are determined by state law. Joint ownership implies two owners, though there are exceptions.

Keogh plan. A retirement savings plan for the self-employed with higher total contribution limits than an IRA.

Letter of Instruction. A Letter of Instruction should contain a complete list of your assets and your wishes about how your estate should be distributed, your funeral conducted, and as much relevant information as you think appropriate. It is a way to help your family when you no longer can.

Levels of care. Terms that outline the type of care a patient needs and, in the case of insurance companies, where treatment is received. There are several levels of care:

basic, custodial, intermediate, personal, skilled, and skilled nursing. Insurers, Medicare, and Medicaid use these terms to calculate payment schedules.

Licensed Practical Nurse (LPN) or Licensed Vocational Nurse (LVN). Nurses who have enough training to be licensed by a state to provide routine care.

Lifestyle mutual funds. Funds that are automatically reviewed annually to consider the owner's financial goals and age. As time passes and the shareholder ages, the mixture of stocks and bonds is adjusted to achieve the best possible return.

Lifetime annuity. A lifetime annuity provides regular payments for your entire life. Payments are fixed (a predetermined amount) or variable (payment amounts may increase or decrease). Because annuity products are so complex, consult a professional before purchasing.

Lifetime maximum benefits. The total amount an insurer will pay for any and all claims made during the life of an insurance policy. If the lifetime maximum is reached on the first claim, the policy expires.

Liquidity. A measure of the expectation of converting an asset to cash. For example, when it is anticipated that an asset, if offered for sale, would be bought quickly and, therefore, easily converted to cash, the asset is said to have "high" liquidity. "Poor" liquidity means just the opposite; an asset would be expected to be on the market for a long time before it was sold and converted to cash.

Living trust. During the term of a living trust, the original owner of the property has control over any funds or property, unless they specify otherwise. The primary reasons to create a trust are its tax implications and to avoid lengthy probate. A trust may reduce or eliminate federal estate taxes for both spouse's estates, while at the same time preserving the asset for the benefit of trust beneficiaries.

Living will. Expresses your wishes regarding your health care once you are in a comatose or vegetative state or are terminally ill, when death is imminent and there is no expectation of recovery, and you are unable to communicate your wishes.

Long-term care. Refers to a comprehensive range of medical, personal, and social services coordinated to meet the physical, social, and emotional needs of the chronically ill or disabled over an indefinite period of time.

Long-term care insurance. Long-term care insurance may expand your service options and choices of facilities. Policies are generally expensive but provide extended benefits for nursing home care, rehabilitation, and other services.

Long-term disability insurance. Benefits are intended to replace lost income during an expected or normal work career. Fixed dollar amounts are paid periodically to cover loss of income during an extended illness or disability.

Major medical or *catastrophic insurance plans.* Cover illnesses or injuries that meet specific criteria.

Markers (grave). All cemeteries and memorial parks or gardens have strict policies on the type, size, and construction of markers. The rule of thumb is that cemeteries allow upright monuments and memorial parks and gardens do not. Some facilities may have zones for different types of markers/monuments.

Mausoleum. An above-ground facility for entombment of remains.

Mediation. Using the services of a professional mediator to reach agreement on divorce issues (except child care and custody).

Medicaid. Medicaid is designed for the low income or medically needy and is sponsored by both federal and state governments. Eligibility requirements differ by state but generally include financial need, recipients under the age of 21 or over 65 or who are blind or disabled.

Medical discharge planner. A person or department at most medical facilities that guide patients and family through their medical stay and assist with discharge procedures.

Medical examiner. A medical examiner is a physician, usually a pathologist.

Medical and surgical insurance plans. Cover physicians services, inpatient, and outpatient service charges, and certain other charges (radiology, laboratory, X-ray) depending on the policy.

Medicare. A government-sponsored health insurance program for U.S. citizens over age 65 or younger with disabilities or those with end-stage renal disease. Younger citizens with physical or mental disadvantages may also be beneficiaries. Medicare covers some skilled nursing and rehabilitative care but generally does not cover custodial care.

Medicare, Part A. Generally covers hospital costs for

medically necessary inpatient services supplied in a hospital or at a skilled nursing facility and for some hospice care.

Medicare, Part B. Generally covers the services of physicians and surgeons and certain other medical services and supplies.

Medicare, Part C. Formerly known as "Medicare+Choice," they are now called "Medicare Advantage" plans and are provided by private insurers.

Medicare, Part D. The Medicare prescription drug plan covers both brand name and generic prescription drugs at participating pharmacies. Medicare prescription drug coverage provides protection for people with very high drug costs. Everyone enrolled in Medicare is eligible for this coverage, regardless of income and resources, health status, or current prescription expenses.

Medicare private fee-for-service plan. A private insurance plan that accepts Medicare participants. Plan members are free to use any Medicare-approved doctor or hospital that accepts the plan. The insurer, rather than Medicare, decides how much and for what services it will reimburse and, consequently, premiums may be high. They may provide other benefits not included in the original Medicare plan (Part A).

Medigap policies. Private insurance companies offer supplemental insurance for coverage of medical costs and expenses not covered by Medicare, Parts A and B.

Money market fund. A mutual fund consisting mainly of short-term debt, usually Treasury bills that mature in one year or less.

Money purchase pension plan. A defined contribution pension plan to which employer contributions are fixed (they may contribute up to 25% of an employee's compensation).

Monuments (grave). All cemeteries and memorial parks or gardens have strict policies on the type, size, and construction of monuments. The rule of thumb is that cemeteries allow upright monuments and memorial parks and gardens do not. Each facility may have zones for different types of markers/monuments.

Municipal bonds. Bonds issued by state and local municipalities to fund projects such as new roads or schools; they are slightly riskier than Treasuries but their tax implications are much broader.

Mutual funds. Mutual funds pool the money of all participants to buy a diverse portfolio of stocks and bonds. Funds are designed to achieve the financial objectives of individuals who otherwise would not or could not participate in the stock market. There are more than 10,000 funds to choose from and their appeal is professional management of your shares.

Niche. A space for an urn in a columbarium or mausoleum.

Nondeductible IRA. The nondeductible IRA is for people who don't qualify for any other IRA or who may only be allowed to make partial contributions. In a nondeductible IRA, money still grows and is tax-deferred until retirement but annual contributions are not tax deductible.

Nondurable power of attorney. A type of power of attorney that lasts until it is revoked or until the person creating it becomes mentally incompetent or dies; unless its terms define specific limits on what it is for, when it will begin, and how long it will last. It is often used for specific transactions.

Nurses aide. An aide assists a nurse in tasks that require little formal training.

Nursing home. A residential assistance facility with varying levels of care for those unable to care for themselves. When selecting a nursing home, consider location, visiting hours, religious affiliation, hospital affiliation, services, and costs.

Obituary. A notice of death published in a newspaper.

Outpatient. A patient admitted to a hospital or clinic who does not require an overnight stay.

Pallbearer. A person carrying or attending a coffin during a funeral.

Parenting coordinator. Helps couples agree on child welfare and support. For divorced or divorcing couples.

Passport. Your passport is an internationally recognized travel document that verifies your identity and nationality. A valid U.S. passport is also required to enter and leave many foreign countries.

Pay-on-death bank account. An account similar to a regular checking account except that is designed to be used by the beneficiary upon the account owner's death. Used as a backup resource for spouses or beneficiaries when other funds are temporarily unavailable.

Pension plan. A traditional pension plan may be sponsored by an employer, union, or joint-trustee (a board that manages the plan), and is regulated by the government. A financial institution usually manages pension plan assets. When you retire, you receive a monthly benefit.

Permanent life insurance plans. An umbrella term for insurance policies that do not expire before death and combine death benefits and savings options. The two main types are "whole" and "universal" life.

Perpetual care. Perpetual care is whatever the cemetery, mausoleum, or columbarium owner says it is. Used for the maintenance and upkeep of the facility as an optional service it is not regulated by law.

Personal care. Assistance with walking, bathing, dressing, and grooming; bowel, bladder, and menstrual care; repositioning or transfer; skin care; range-of-motion exercises; feeding, hydration; and help with self-administered medications.

Personal emergency medical response system. An emergency medical response system installed in the home that may be purchased, rented, or leased. It consists of a wireless radio transmitter worn by the user to contact a monitoring center via a landline telephone. Used by elderly living alone or those with chronic illnesses.

Personal report. Obtained from a reputable private investigative firm that includes credit, legal, and other personal information.

Policy maximum benefits. Policy maximum benefit refers to the total dollar amounts for individual items indentified in the policy that will be paid under any insurance policy. Once the policy maximum benefit has been reached, the insurer will stop payment on that treatment service, test, etc.

Power of attorney. A legal tool that designates another

person to handle your affairs. It does not mean that you cannot make your own decisions or control your own affairs. You are sharing power—not giving it away. With an attorney, any competent adult may create a power of attorney, limit what may be transacted, and revoke it at any time for any reason.

Power of attorney for finances. A legal tool that designates another person to handle your financial affairs. It does not mean that you cannot make your own decisions or control your own affairs. You are sharing power—not giving it away. With an attorney, any competent adult may create a power of attorney for finances that may (or may not) identify exactly what financial transactions may be performed, and that may be revoked at any time for any reason.

Premium. The payment for an insurance policy or annuity.

Prenuptial Agreement. Defines how mutual and separate assets, debts, income, and other financial and personal items and responsibilities will be handled before, during, and after a marriage.

Private Mortgage Insurance (PMI). Insurance required by the lender that you pay for and that is administered by a private insurer. In most states, private mortgage insurance is required if you have not put down 20% or more on an initial mortgage. PMI is calculated on ½ of a percent of the total loan amount and is collected until your equity reaches 20% of the original loan. You may prepay PMI and you certainly do not want it included in your mortgage payments. Lenders are legally required to automatically stop collecting PMI payments when your equity reaches 20%.

Probate. Probate is a court process to settle an estate. A will is submitted to the court and a petition for probate is filed. A hearing determines if the will is valid. Notice is given to all heirs and creditors and is published in the local newspapers. The court appoints an administrator, executor (male) or executrix (female) of the estate (usually the one named in the will). During probate, creditors have several months to file claims (liens) against the estate. All assets are appraised and debts paid. Once all debts have been paid and the time for filing creditor claims has expired, another petition is filed with the court seeking its approval to close the probate, pay the attorney, and distribute the estate. This process takes a minimum of six months. Each state has its own laws and not every estate needs to be probated.

Profit-sharing pension plan. Most profit-sharing pension plans allow you to receive benefits when you reach a specified age (usually retirement age, 65), after a specified number of years of employment, or you become disabled or terminate.

Program of All-Inclusive Care for the Elderly (PACE). Combines medical, social, and long-term care services and is only available in some states under Medicaid. The goal of PACE is to help people remain independent and live in their community as long as possible while receiving high-quality care. To be eligible, you must be 55 years of age or older, live within the PACE service area, be certified by an appropriate state agency as eligible for nursing home care, and be able to live safely in the community.

Promissory note. A simple form signed and dated by

the lender and the borrower that indicates what is borrowed, how, and when repayment will be made, interest rate (if any), and identifies collateral (if any). It is a legal contract and any interest charged may not be more than your state's legal rate.

Qualified domestic relations order. To make sure pension plans recognize your rights to a portion of your spouse's pension after a divorce, you need to obtain a separate court order. When the court issues a qualified domestic relations order awarding you a share of your spouse's pension, a copy must be immediately sent to the pension plan provider. The provider will want to make sure of two things: (1) that the court order contains all the necessary information so that they can determine who, what, and when to pay; and (2) that the court order does not require the plan to pay in a way or at a time that would not otherwise be permitted. For example, a court cannot order a plan to pay a lump sum if the plan does not allow other employees to draw their pensions this way.

Qualified joint and survivor option. An annuity option that allows a beneficiary to receive between 50% and 100% of the annuity benefits following the death of the purchaser. The point is to safeguard the money you've paid in by assuring that your spouse receives whatever you do not. Without the qualified joint and survivor option, payments would stop at the death of the person who purchased the annuity.

Registered Nurse (RN). An RN is a professional nurse who supervises the tasks performed by Licensed Practical Nurses, Licensed Vocational Nurses, orderlies, and nursing aides. They provide direct care and make decisions regarding plans of care for individuals and groups of healthy, ill, and injured people and have many hours of clinical experience.

Respite care. As its name implies, it is at-home or at-hospice care given to patients to alleviate the burden on the usual caregiver. If you are the primary caregiver, respite caregivers step in and take over your responsibilities to give you a break.

Reverse mortgage. For homeowners age 62 or more who wish to borrow against the equity in their homes. It pays the homeowner a line of credit, lump sum, or series of monthly payments. The homeowner does not repay it as long as they live in the home. The loan is repaid when the owner no longer occupies the home and the lender sells it to recover their money.

Revocable Trust. Allows the grantor the option to revoke or change the terms of a trust as desired.

Rider. An insurance rider is a provision or modification to an existing policy that provides additional coverage. Generally, riders are sold separately and may include coverage to pay an accelerated death benefit, to add children to a life policy, or to include specific items. Double indemnity riders pay twice the amount of the policy if you die accidentally.

Roll over. When you leave an employer, you may roll over (or move) your mutual funds, IRA, 401(k), and Health Savings Account to the new one. To minimize any loss of funds in the process or incur tax penalties, you need professional advice. The Benefits Officers at your former (and new) employer will be able to help. If you are only moving your IRA from one employer's financial institution to another, consider a transfer that is not subject to IRS reporting. Roll overs must be completed within sixty days.

Roth IRA. A Roth IRA provides tax benefits at retirement rather than up front. Contributions cannot be deducted on your annual income tax return, but when you begin withdrawing funds at age 59½, you will not pay taxes. Roth IRAs are available to everyone, whether or not you have a company retirement plan. Roth IRAs have income requirements and contribution limits.

Senior daycare. For seniors with Alzheimer's or other types of dementia.

Service-related disability compensation. Veterans' compensation paid monthly depending on the disability or disease that was developed or aggravated during service. The amount of compensation is based on the effects and severity of the disability or disease and number of dependents.

Short-term care. The length of time medical services will be needed; usually 90 days or less.

Simplified Employee Pension (SEP-IRA). Simplified Employee Pension funds are IRAs designed for self-employed individuals as well as small business owners and their employees. Contributions to SEP-IRAs are immediately 100% vested.

Single-ownership asset. Usually, a person owns property after having purchased it using only their own income earned while residing in either a community property state or a non-community property state. They may use the property for pleasure or profit and dispose of it as they choose. They are responsible for all expenses and other charges, such as taxes. Check your state laws for their definition.

Skilled care. Requires the services of registered nurses and other specially trained professionals for treatments and procedures on a regular basis. Skilled care is continuous, all-day care.

Skilled nursing care. Care supervised by registered nurses. Examples of services include intravenous injections, maintaining feeding tubes, oxygen, and changing sterile dressings. A skilled nursing care facility is staffed and equipped for rehabilitation and other related health services.

Social adult daycare. An adult daycare facility that usually requires a physician's health assessment for admission.

Social Managed Care plans. HMO insurance plans that provide a full range of Medicare benefits. There are four Social Managed Care plans: Kaiser Permanente (Portland, OR); SCAN (Long Beach, CA); Elderplan (Brooklyn, NY); and Health Plan of Nevada (Las Vegas, NV). Plan participants must use specific doctors, specialists, and/or hospitals. Plans cover all Medicare, Parts A (hospital) and B (medical), services and some include prescription drugs coverage. Generally less expensive than private insurance and may or may not cover nursing home care.

Social Security. Social Security is a U.S. Government-sponsored insurance program providing not only retirement income but disability insurance and survivor's benefits for children and spouses. You earn Social Security credits when you pay into the system at your place of employment. Benefits may be taxable depending on your total income.

Social Worker. A professional trained to help individuals and their families with emotional or physical needs and assist with support services.

Socially responsible mutual fund (or ethical fund). This type of mutual fund only invests in companies that meet certain guidelines and most do not invest in industries such as tobacco, alcohol, weapons, or nuclear power.

Specialty mutual fund. Specialty mutual funds concentrate their investments in certain segments of the economy (financial, technology, health, for example). Also known as "sector funds."

Specified disease insurance plan. Pays the insured a fixed, flat amount for each day of hospitalization for specific condition(s) or disease(s).

Spousal consent form. If you are married when your spouse retires, you are usually entitled to survivor's benefits from pension plans upon the death of your spouse. It is important to remember that, statistically, wives are likely to outlive husbands and therefore need more income for a longer retirement. A spousal consent form assures that any survivor benefits are paid to the surviving spouse. The last chance you have to make sure that your spouse receives survivor's benefits is at the time of your retirement.

Spousal IRA. Allows full-time homemakers or spouses with little or no income to contribute to a savings plan.

Springing power of attorney. Same as other powers of attorney but relies on a particular event or events to become effective. The person creating the power of attorney may designate what event or events must occur before the power of attorney becomes effective. May be revoked at any time for any reason.

Stock. Stocks represent ownership in a company. Stocks are traded in units called "shares."

Stock bonus plans. Stock bonus plans are profit-sharing plans that deliver benefits to employees in the form of stock rather than cash. Stock bonus plans may be deferred to retirement.

Subsidized Senior Housing (non-medical). Federal and state programs available for elder housing for those with low to moderate incomes. Some subsidized facilities offer assistance with certain tasks, such as shopping and laundry. Residents generally live independently in an apartment within the senior housing complex with communal dining.

Successor trustee. A subordinate trustee of a trust. They act as backup for the designated trustee.

Supplemental Social Security Income. Originally designated for widows and orphans, Supplemental Social Security Income now pays benefits to people over 65 years of age who have very little income or to younger low-income, disabled people.

Survivor's benefits. The survivor's benefits of some retirement plans are converted to joint survivor annuities and ordinarily guarantee that the surviving spouse continues to receive half (or more) of the pension benefits. Read the company's pension plan booklet carefully and consult the plan administrator.

Term life insurance. Provides coverage for a specific period of time; if not renewed the policy lapses. A term life policy may be renewed for the same number of years as the original policy, although then premiums may be higher.

Testamentary trust. A trust established in a will. May not be altered or revoked and is subject to probate.

Testator. The person making a will.

Traditional funeral service. Traditional services may include a casket, viewing hours, a formal funeral service (at the funeral parlor and/or religious site and/or interment site), use of a hearse and other vehicles, graveside service, and/or cremation.

Treasuries. Include Treasury Bills or "T-bills" (mature in ninety days to a year); Treasury Notes (mature in two to ten years); and Treasury Bonds (mature in ten or more years). Treasury securities are debt instruments; that is, when you buy the bonds offered by the U.S. Government, it uses the money to pay the bills of operating the country. For the use of the money, the government pays interest and returns all the money when the bond matures. They are considered very safe investments because they are backed by the "full faith and credit" of the U.S. Government.

Trust. A legal arrangement created for the ownership and management of real property, cash or investments, or other assets that are eventually distributed to trust beneficiaries.

Trust assets. Any asset put in trust is owned by the trust. Examples of trust assets may be cash, homes, rental property, mutual funds, art, or collectibles. To put property, for example, a condo, in trust, the name of the owner on the condo deed must be changed to the name of the trust. Any income from property in a trust belongs to the trust.

Trustee. A person who manages a trust.

Unfunded trust. An unfunded trust may just be the paperwork to create a trust and may be considered a viable trust for some time after it is created even though it doesn't have anything in it; it is designated to receive assets in the future. However, in some states, a nominal funding (say, $100) is required to legally establish a trust.

Universal life insurance. A permanent life plan providing coverage during the insured's life that has a savings element. Universal life plans accumulate cash value through the investment of premiums. Policyholders are allowed to use the earnings on current premiums to pay future premiums. Premiums, benefit payments, and benefit payment schedules are variable and rely on interest rates and the performance of the investments. Death benefits, premiums, and savings may be reviewed and altered as the policyholder's circumstances change.

Variable life insurance. A type of whole life insurance for which some or all of the premiums are invested by the insurer and the amount of the death benefit depends on the performance of the investments.

Variable universal life insurance. A type of whole life insurance for which premiums are invested by the insurer and the amount of the death benefit depends on the performance of the investments. However, while the insurance company places some or all of the fixed premium payments into an investment account, they may require that the policyholder decide how the money is invested. In this way, the policyholder bears the risk and responsibility for any investment losses, and any resulting reduction in the death benefit amount, though there is a guaranteed minimum benefit payment.

Vault. An outside container that surrounds a casket in concrete or other material to minimize ground settling. Some cemeteries require vaults while others require grave liners and yet others accept both.

Vesting. Employer pension plans require that employees reach a set number of months or years of employment before being entitled to participate in pension benefits. Exact requirements are specified in the plan terms. Vesting occurs when the employee completes the required service.

Veteran. Any person who has served in any branch of the United States Armed Forces.

Veterans health care benefits. The Veterans Administration provides a comprehensive range of medical benefits including outpatient services, hospitalization, home and respite care, nursing home care, long-term care, dental care, and hearing and vision aids. Some veterans are automatically eligible for VA health care benefits and others must apply for them.

Will. A will is a set of instructions describing how property will be handled after death.

Whole life insurance (also called straight life or ordinary life). A whole life insurance policy provides coverage during the insured's lifetime. Whole life policies build cash reserves that may be paid to the policyholder when they surrender, or partially surrender, the policy or use the cash reserves to fund low-interest loans.

Appendix

Emergency Communication Plan.

The U.S. Government Office for Homeland Security website (www.ready.gov) also has other important information.

Homeland Security Family Communications Plan

Your family may not be together when disaster strikes, so plan how you will contact one another and review what you will do in different situations.

Out-of-Town Contact Name: _____
Phone Number: _____
Email: _____
Address: _____

Fill out the following information for each family member and keep it up to date.

Name: _____

Social Security Number: _____

Date of Birth: _____

Important Medical Information _____

Name: _____

Social Security Number: _____

Date of Birth: _____

Important Medical Information _____

Name: _____

Social Security Number: _____

Date of Birth: _____

Important Medical Information _____

Name: _____

Social Security Number: _____

Date of Birth: _____

Important Medical Information _____

Name: _____

Social Security Number: _____

Date of Birth: _____

Important Medical Information _____

Name: _____

Social Security Number: _____

Date of Birth: _____

Important Medical Information _____

Where to go in an emergency. Write down where your family spends the most time: work, school and other places you frequent. Schools, daycare providers, workplaces and apartment buildings should all have site-specific emergency plans.

Home
Address:_____

Phone Number: _____

Neighborhood Meeting Place: _____

School
Address:_____

Phone Number: _____

Evacuation Location: _____

School
Address:_____

Phone Number: _____

Evacuation Location: _____

School
Address:_____

Phone Number: _____

Evacuation Location: _____

Dad's Work
Address:_____

Phone Number: _____

Evacuation Location: _____

Regional Meeting Place:_____

Mom's Work _____

Address: _____

Phone Number: _____

Evacuation Location: _____

Regional Meeting Place: _____

_____

Other places you frequent:

Address: _____

Phone Number: _____

Evacuation Location: _____

Address: _____

Phone Number: _____

EvacuationLocation: _____

_____

Other Information

Name: _____

Phone: _____

Doctor(s): _____

Other: _____

Pharmacist: _____

Medical Insurance: _____

Policy: _____

Homeowners/Rental Insurance: _____

Veterinarian/Kennel: _____

Other useful phone numbers:

9-1-1 for emergencies.

Police Non-Emergency Phone:

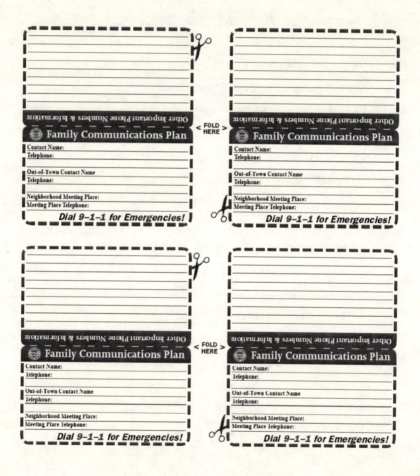

EMERGENCY PHONE NUMBERS

You may also wish to include the phone numbers of the gas and electric companies, the local pharmacy, and who has copies of the list.

911
_____

Police: _____

Fire: _____

Nearest hospital:
Name: _____
Address: _____
Phone: _____

Doctor:
Name: _____
Phone: _____

Pharmacy:
Name: _____
Phone: _____

Poison Control:
1-800-222-1222

Ambulance:

Name_____

Phone_____

Insurance co.:

Name_____

Phone_____

Insurance Policy number:

_____

FAMILY

_____

Dad's Work number: _____

Dad's Cell number: _____

Mom's Work number: _____

Mom's Cell number: _____

CHILDREN:

_____

Child's name:_____

Date of birth: _____

Bloodtype: _____

School: _____

Name: _____

Address:_____

Phone: _____

School contact:

Name_____

Phone_____

Allergies:

Medications:

Medical conditions:

Child's name:_____

Date of birth: _____

Bloodtype: _____

School: _____

Name: _____

Address:_____

Phone: _____

School contact:

Name: _____

Phone:_____

CONTACTS

Emergency contact name:

Name: _____

Address: _____

Phone: _____

Contact's relationship:

Contact phone: _____

Contact cell: _____

Caregiver name:

Caregiver phone: _____

Caregiver cell: _____

Caregiver address: _____

MEMBERSHIP LIST

Organization	Address

Primary Contact Name/Phone	Membership Number

ASSET LIST

Asset	Date Acquired	Cost	Warranty	Warranty Expiration	Notes	Cuurent fair Market Value
Kitchen						
Living Room						
Den						
Library						
Bedroom 1						

Asset	Date Acquired	Cost	Warranty	Warranty Expiration	Notes	Cuurent fair Market Value
Bedroom 2						
Bedroom 3						
Bedroom 4						
Garage						
Cars						
Boats						

Asset	Date Acquired	Cost	Warranty	Warranty Expiration	Notes	Cuurent fair Market Value
Collectibles						
Antiques						

EXAMPLE OF A DURABLE POWER OF ATTORNEY

Do not execute any power of attorney without the advice of an attorney.

I, [full legal name], residing at [full address], appoint [name of agent] of [agent's address and phone], as my attorney-in-fact ("agent"). If my agent is unable to serve, I designate [name], of [address and phone], as successor agent.

I hereby revoke any and all powers of attorney previously signed by me. This power of attorney shall become effective immediately and shall not be affected by my disability or lack of mental competence, except as provided by state statute. It shall continue effective until my death.

My agent has full authority to act on my behalf to manage and conduct my affairs and exercise all of my legal rights. These powers shall include but are not limited to:

Banking

Sell, exchange, buy, invest, or reinvest any of my assets or property.

Sell, convey, lease, mortgage, manage, insure, improve, repair my property.

Enter into binding contracts on my behalf.

Purchase and/or maintain all insurance policies.

Collect my debts or settle any claims.

Manage all stock or other investments.

Maintain and/or operate my business.

Prepare, sign, and file documents with any government agency.

Make gifts from my assets except my agent may not make gifts of my property or assets to himself.

Listing specific powers does not limit or restrict those granted in this power of attorney.

My agent shall not be liable for any loss that results from a judgment error made in good faith. They shall be liable for willful misconduct or failing to act in good faith. I authorize my agent to indemnify and hold harmless any third party who accepts and acts under this document.

My agent shall provide an accounting for all funds handled and all acts performed.

This document does not authorize any medical and other health care decisions.

[date] _____, at

[address] _____.

Your signature: _____

Your printed name: _____

Witness signature   Witness signature

_____   _____

Witness printed name   Witness printed name

_____   _____

Notary Public seal

EXAMPLE OF A POWER OF ATTORNEY FOR HEALTH CARE

Do not execute any power of attorney without the advice of an attorney.

I, [name], am of sound mind and voluntarily make this designation. I appoint [name], living at [address and phone], as my agent to make care, custody, and medical treatment decisions for me in the event I become unable to participate in these decisions, including treatment decisions that would allow my death, and I fully understand that such decisions could or would allow my death.

1. This power of attorney for health care will not become effective unless I am unable to participate in treatment decisions.
2. My agent will not exercise any powers concerning care, custody, and medical treatment that I could not.
3. My agent will act ethically and in my best interests and in accordance with my wishes.
4. I may revoke this designation at any time.
    I designate [name of successor agent] living at [address and phone] as my successor agent.
    Signed: _____
    Date: _____
    Address: _____
    Witnesses

Two (or three in some states) adult witnesses. One witness may not be a beneficiary of your will; may not be your spouse or a relative; and is not your physician, an employee of your physician, or an employee of the health care facility where you are a patient.

Witness Statement

I declare that this power of attorney was signed in my presence by [name] who appears to be of sound mind, making this designation voluntarily and without duress, fraud, or undue influence.

Signed by witness: _____

(Print full name) _____

Address: _____

Signed by witness: _____

(Print full name) _____

Address: _____

Signed by witness: _____

(Print full name) _____

Address: _____

Agent acceptance: I understand the above conditions and I accept the appointment of agent.

Agent [Name] _____

Dated: _____Signed: _____

EXAMPLE OF A SIMPLE LIVING WILL

Do not execute any will without the advice of an attorney.

I, [name], am of sound mind and voluntarily make this living will. I understand its meaning, accept its consequences, and have signed it after careful consideration.

If I am terminally ill or permanently unconscious as determined by my doctor [name] and at least one other doctor, and unable to participate in decisions regarding medical treatment, this living will is to be honored as the expression of my legal right to consent to or refuse medical treatment.

My wishes for medical treatment are:

_____

_____

_____

I am solely responsible for these directives and no civil or criminal liability for following my wishes shall be attached to any caregiver.

As long as I can communicate in any manner, this living will does not become effective.

Signed: _____ Dated: _____

Address: _____

This declaration was signed in our presence by

[name] who appears to be of sound mind and making it voluntarily without duress, fraud, or undue influence.

Signed by witness: _____

Address: _____

Signed by witness: _____

Address: _____

Signed by witness: _____

Address: _____

LIVING WILL QUESTIONS

To help clarify your thinking on medical issues, review the following items. The care you want is as important as what you do not want.

* Your religious beliefs

* Organ and tissue donation

* Your views on living independently and quality of life

* In the case of coma and/or brain damage, review each question and the four answers to each:

If I am in a coma and have no chance of waking up?
If I am in a coma from which I may awaken?
If I have brain damage?
If I have a terminal illness?

　　I want treatment.

WHEN LIFE CHANGES FOREVER

Try the treatment but if I do not clearly improve, stop.
I do not know if I want treatment.
I do not want treatment.

   *Medical treatments that may or may not be acceptable:

Antibiotics
Blood transfusions
Chemotherapy
CPR (re-starting your heart and breathing)
Invasive tests
Surgery
Tubes or IV's for food or fluids
Ventilator

To combine the characteristics of a power of attorney for health care and a living will, you may designate an agent on your living will. To do so, you may add language such as:

I appoint [name], living at [address], as my agent to make care, custody, and medical treatment decisions for me in the event I become unable to participate in these decisions, including treatment decisions that would allow my death, and I fully understand that such decisions could or would allow my death.

My agent will not exercise any powers concerning care, custody, and medical treatment that I could not and will act ethically and in my best interests and in accordance with my wishes.

These are only suggestions; if you need help, ask your physician, or get a form from your physician or local hospital that may contain other issues you may wish to consider.

EXAMPLE OF A PROMISSORY NOTE

A Promissory Note is a legal contract; do not execute one without the advice of an attorney.

Date _____

Borrower: _____

Borrower's Address: _____

$ _____

Payee: _____

Place for Payment: _____

Principal Amount: _____

Interest rate _____

Term: _____

Monthly Payments: $_____

Final payment due: _____

Borrower is responsible for all obligations represented by this note.

Payment terms. This Note is due and payable as defined above. The first payment is due and payable on [insert day, month, year], and subsequent installments are due and payable on the same day of each succeeding month until the total principal is repaid. If a payment is not made on time, the remaining balance will be due immediately and subject to the interest stated above [*may not be greater than allowed in the state in which the note is executed*].

Pre-payment. Borrower reserves the right to prepay this Note in whole or in part, without penalty. Any unpaid amounts are due on the final scheduled payment date.

Default. If Borrower defaults on this Note, Payee may declare the unpaid principal and interest due immediately.

Form of payment. Check, cash, Money Order, or other means acceptable to the holder.

Attorney's fees. If this Note is turned over to an attorney for collection or enforcement, or if suit is brought for collection or enforcement, or it must be collected or enforced through probate, bankruptcy, or other judicial proceeding, the Borrower shall pay for all processing fees in addition to other amounts due.

Governing law. This Note is governed, construed, and interpreted by, through, and under the Laws of the State of _____

Executed this _____ day of _____, 200_____.

Borrower's Signature: _____

Borrower's Printed or Typed Name: _____

BANKRUPTCY: TWO-MINUTE WARNING

Living/debt ratio: Rent = mortgage or rental payments (30%) and debt payments (28%) (debts are loans, not living expenses).

	Cost	
Rent	$	
Mortgage	$	
Total A		$
Car payment	$	
Student loans	$	
Other loans	$	
Total B		$
Income		$
Divide Total A by income	%	Should not be more than 30%
Divide Total B by income	%	Should not be more than 28%

FUNERAL GENERAL PRICE LIST: FOUR EXAMPLES

The following sample general price lists will give you an idea of what goods and services are provided. They are only basic examples and will differ from what an individual funeral provider offers. They are excerpted from the Federal Trade Commission, "Complying with the Funeral Rule," www.ftc.gov, accessed 3/17/07.

EXAMPLE 1: BASIC PRODUCTS AND SERVICES PRICE LIST

GENERAL PRICE LIST

These prices are effective as of [date].

The goods and services shown below are those we can provide to our customers. You may choose only the items you desire. However, any funeral arrangements you select will include a charge for our basic services and overhead. If legal or other requirements mean you must buy any items you did not specifically ask for, we will explain the reason in writing on the statement we provide describing the funeral goods and services you selected.

Basic Services of Funeral Director and Staff and Overhead .... $ ———

This fee for our basic services and overhead will be added to the total cost of the funeral arrangements you select. (This fee is already included in our charges for direct cremations, immediate burials, and forwarding or receiving remains.) Our services include: conducting the arrangements conference; planning the funeral; consulting with family and clergy; sheltering remains; preparing and filing of necessary notices; obtaining necessary authorizations and permits; coordinating with the cemetery, crematory, or other third parties.

Embalming .... $_____

Except in certain special cases, embalming is not required by law. Embalming may be necessary, however, if you select certain funeral arrangements, such as a funeral with viewing. If you do not want embalming, you usually have the right to choose an arrangement that does not require it, such as direct cremation or immediate burial.

Other Preparation of the Body .... $ _____

List all services and prices (for example cosmetology, dressing, etc.)

Transfer of Remains to the Funeral Home (within _____ mile radius) .... $ _____

Beyond this radius we charge _____ per mile.

Use of Facilities and Staff for Viewing at the Funeral Home .... $ _____

Use of Facilities and Staff for Funeral Ceremony at the Funeral Home .... $ _____

Use of Facilities and Staff for Memorial Service at the Funeral Home .... $ _____

Use of Equipment and Staff for Graveside Service
.... _____

Hearse .... $ _____

Limousine.. $ _____

Caskets .... $ _____ to $ _____

A complete price list for caskets will be provided at the funeral home.

Outer Burial Containers $ _____ to $ _____

A complete price list of burial containers will be provided at the funeral home.

Forwarding of Remains to Another Funeral Home .... $ _____

Our charge includes basic services of funeral director and staff, a proportionate share of overhead costs, removal of remains, embalming or other preparation of remains if relevant, and local transportation.

Receiving Remains from Another Funeral Home .... $ _____

Our charge includes basic services of funeral director and staff, a proportionate share of overhead costs, care of remains, transportation of remains to funeral home and to cemetery or crematory.

Direct Cremation .... $ _____ to $ _____

Our charge for a direct cremation (without ceremony) includes: basic services of funeral director and staff; a proportionate share of overhead costs; removal of remains; transportation to crematory; necessary authorizations; and cremation, if relevant.

For a direct cremation, you can use an alternative container. Alternative containers encase the body and can be made of materials like fiberboard or composition materials (with or without an outside covering). The containers we provide are a fiberboard container or an unfinished wood box.

A. Direct cremation with container provided by the purchaser..$ _____

B. Direct cremation with a fiberboard container.
....$ _____

C. Direct cremation with an unfinished wood box
....$ _____

Immediate Burial...........$ _____ to $_____

Our charge for an immediate burial (without ceremony) includes basic services of funeral director and staff, a proportionate share of overhead costs, removal of remains, and local transportation to cemetery.

A. Immediate burial with casket provided by purchaser..$ _____

B. Immediate burial with alternative container [if offered] ....$ _____

C. Immediate burial with cloth-covered wood casket ....$ _____

EXAMPLE 2: CASKET PRICE LIST

These prices are effective as of [date].

Alternative Containers

1. Fiberboard Box .... $ _____
2. Plywood Box .... $ _____
3. Unfinished Pine Box .... $ _____

Caskets

1. Beige cloth-covered soft-wood with beige interior .... $ _____
2. Oak-stained soft-wood with pleated blue crepe interior... $ _____
3. Mahogany-finished soft-wood with maroon crepe interior... $ _____

EXAMPLE 3: OUTER BURIAL CONTAINER PRICE LIST

These prices are effective as of [date].

In most areas of the country, state or local law does not require that you buy a container to surround the casket in the grave. However, many cemeteries require that you have such a container so that the grave will not sink in. Either a grave liner or a burial vault will satisfy these requirements.

1. Concrete Grave Liner.......................... $ _____
2. Acme Reinforced Concrete Vault (lined) .... $ _____

3. Acme Reinforced Concrete Vault (stainless steel lined) .... $ _____

EXAMPLE 4: STATEMENT OF PRODUCTS AND SERVICES SELECTED

Charges are only for those items that you select or that are required. If we are required by law or by a cemetery or crematory to use any items, we will explain the reasons in writing below.

Basic Services of Funeral Director and Staff and Overhead .... $ _____
Embalming .... $ _____
If you selected a funeral that may require embalming, such as a funeral with viewing, you may have to pay for embalming. You do not have to pay for embalming you did not approve if you selected arrangements such as a direct cremation or immediate burial. If we charged for embalming, we will explain why below.
Other Preparation of the Body
1. Cosmetic Work for Viewing .... $ _____
2. Washing and Disinfecting Unembalmed Remains .... $ _____
Transfer of Remains to the Funeral Home ....
.... $ _____
Use of Facilities and Staff for Viewing ... $ _____
Use of Facilities and Staff for Funeral Ceremony
.... $ _____

Use of Facilities and Staff for Memorial Service.
.... $ _____

Use of Equipment and Staff for Graveside Service.
.... $ _____

Hearse... $ _____

Limousine.. $ _____

Casket.. $ _____

Outer Burial Container.......................... $ _____

Forwarding Remains to Another Funeral Home
.... $ _____

Receiving Remains from Another Funeral Home
.... $ _____

Direct Cremation.................................. $ _____

Immediate Burial .... $ _____

Cash-Advance Items: We charge you for our services in obtaining:

Cemetery charges.................................. $ _____

Crematory charges .... $ _____

Flowers .... $ _____

Obituary notice..................................... $ _____

Death certificate................................... $ _____

Music.. $ _____

Other.. $ _____

Total Cash-Advance Items..................... $ _____

Total Cost of Arrangements.................... $ _____
(including all services, merchandise, and cash-advance items)

If any legal, cemetery, or crematory requirement

has required the purchase of any of the items listed above, we will explain the requirement below.

Reason for Embalming:

_____

EXAMPLE OF WILL PREPARATION ITEMS

List the contents of your estate, whether held individually or jointly. These are only examples of items to think about. Estimate values or leave them off; when you meet with an attorney to execute your will, you will need specific numbers.

Beneficiaries/Heirs
  Spouse: _____
  Children
    1. _____
    2. _____
    3. _____
    4. _____
  Others
    1. _____
    2. _____
    3. _____
    4. _____
Executrix or Executor
    1. _____
    2. _____

Successors

1. _____

2. _____

Bank Accounts

1. _____ $ _____

2. _____ $ _____

3. _____ $ _____

4. _____ $ _____

Annuities, certificates of deposit, stocks, bonds, Treasuries, others

1. _____ $ _____

2. _____ $ _____

3. _____ $ _____

4. _____ $ _____

Life insurance, IRAs, pensions, 401(k)s, Health Savings Accounts, others

1. _____ $ _____

2. _____ $ _____

3. _____ $ _____

4. _____ $ _____

Real Estate

1. _____ $ _____

2. _____ $ _____

Personal property (*furniture, jewelry, art, or anything else of significant real or emotional value that you wish to pass on to a particular person or organization*)

1. _____
2. _____
3. _____
4. _____

Charities (*bequests to charitable organizations may reduce the taxes on your estate*)

1. _____
2. _____
3. _____
4. _____

RESOURCE *Directory*

In what follows, the extension ".gov" indicates a government resource; ".org" indicates a non-profit operation; and ".com" indicates a commercial operation. This is pointed out only because .gov's and .org's are unlikely to try to sell you something.

EMERGENCY PLANS

American Red Cross: www.redcross.org
U.S. Department of Homeland Security: www.ready.gov/america/makeaplan/index.html
Vital records: National Center for Health Statistics www.cdc.gov (type in *vital records* in the Search block.

ADVISORS/PLANNERS

Financial: www.mymoney.gov; the American Association of Retired Persons (AARP) has a wonderful website at www.aarp.org; 360 Degress of Financial Literacy for Women sponsored by the American Institute of Certified Public Accountants at www.360financialliteracy.org; and American Consumer Credit Counseling at www.consumer-credit.com, are all excellent.

Medical: the AARP website at www.aarp.org, and depending on what you are looking for, there are any number of websites on particular illnesses and disabilities. Always confirm the information with your doctor or local American Medical Association.

Insurance: the AARP website at www.aarp.org. Few major insurers provide informative online resources. MetLife at www.metlife.com is the exception with an understandable and comprehensive array of general information and information on their products. But, of course, we did not review every website.

Legal: www.Nolo.com. There are many "legal" websites out there, most are sales sites.

BANKRUPTCY

An informative site is the U.S. Trustee Program at the U.S. Department of Justice, www.usdoj.gov/ust. Search *bankruptcy* at www.MyMoney.gov for more information.

BUDGETING

www.MyMoney.gov is an excellent source.

CAREGIVER SUPPORT

Full Circle of Care: www.fullcirclecare.org
Assisted living facilities: Administration on Aging (www.aoa.gov);
Assisted Living Federation of America (www.alfa.org); and the National Center for Assisted Living (www.ncal.org). At www.medicare.gov search

caregiver or *assisted living, board care, community service locator,* and *continuing care retirement communities.*

CREDIT REPORTS

At the Federal Trade Commission, www.ftc.gov/, go to "Consumers" and "Credit."

For a free annual credit report visit www.annualcreditreport.com or call 1–877–322–8228 or write to:
Annual Credit Report Request Service
P. O. Box 105283
Atlanta, GA 30348–5281

ELDERCARE LOCATOR

Administration on Aging, Department of Health and Human Services has information on help for elders in your location, 1–800–677–1116 or visit www.eldercare.gov.

FUNERAL

At the Federal Trade Commission web site, www.ftc.gov, search *funeral* and notice the booklet entitled: *Paying Final Respects: Your Rights When Buying Funeral Goods and Services.*

HOME HEALTH CARE COMPARE

See Medicare's page at
www.medicaregovHHCompare/Home.asp

HOSPITAL (FIND A HOSPITAL)

The U.S. Department of Health and Human Services offers comparisons of hospitals caring for certain Medicare conditions; see www.hospitalcompare.hhs.gov/hospital/home2.asp.

Hospital Compare. To compare hospitals in your area for all their adult patients with certain medical conditions. www.hospitalcompare.hhs.gov
To compare quality by facility, visit www.qualitycheck.org. It may also be used to find hospital and medical suppliers in your area.

INSURANCE

An excellent source of information is Consumer Reports, www.consumerreports.org.

MEDICARE

The Health Assistance Partnership, www.healthassistancepartnership.org/

The Centers for Medicare and Medicaid at the U.S. Department of Health and Human Services, www.cms.hhs.gov.
Medicare booklets can be found at www.medicare.gov/publications.
For a Medicare glossary of terms, see www.medicare.gov and search *glossary*.

MEDICARE ADVOCACY

The Center for Medicare Advocacy, Inc., publishes a variety of materials on Medicare, Medigap, and Medicaid, including how to pursue a Medicare appeal or home health care appeal at www.medicareadvocacy.org or

Center for Medicare Advocacy, Inc.
P.O. Box 350
Willimantic, CT 06226
(860) 456–7790.

NURSING HOMES

The online page of *MyZiva,* a nursing home business magazine, can be found at www.myziva.net; and www.seniors.gov is a Senior Citizen Resource sponsored by USA.gov.

NURSING HOMES COMPARE

See Medicare's page at www.medicare.gov and search *nursing home compare.*

NURSING HOMES INSPECTIONS

To learn more about nursing home inspections, see: www.medicare.gov/Nursing/AboutInspections.asp

PACE Program
See www.cms.hhs.gov/PACE/

TRUSTS

Search *trusts* at www.metlife.com.

STATE HEALTH INSURANCE ASSISTANCE PROGRAM

Every state has a State Health Insurance Assistance Program offering free help to Medicare beneficiaries and their families with health insurance choices and other issues. To find the program office in your location, go to www.healthassistancepartnership. org/ and search for *State Health Insurance Programs.*

National Academy of Elder Law Attorneys, Inc.
1604 N. Country Club Road
Tucson, AZ 85716
(520) 881–4005; fax: (520) 325–7925
www.naela.com

American Bar Association Commission on Legal Problems of the Elderly
740 15th Street, NW
Washington, DC 20005–1022
(202) 662–1000
www.abanet.org, click on *Find Legal Help* provides legal resources by state.